The Secret Investing Book

SECOND EDITION

By Christopher M. Uhl, CMA

The Top 100 People in Finance,
Host of How To Trade Stocks and Options Podcast
OVTLYR.COM

Table of Contents

Disclaimer

NO INVESTMENT ADVICE. The information available through the Service is for general informational purposes only and references to specific securities, investment programs or funds are only for illustrative or educational purposes.

No portion of the Service is a solicitation, recommendation, endorsement, or offer by OVTLYR or any third-party service provider to buy or sell any securities or financial instruments. You should not construe any such information or other material on the Service as legal, tax, investment, financial, or other advice.

OVTLYR is not a fiduciary by virtue of any person's use of the Service. You alone assume the sole responsibility for evaluating the merits and risks associated with your use of any information on the Service. Nothing herein constitutes an offer or a solicitation of the purchase or sale of any security to any person in any jurisdiction in which such an offer or solicitation is not authorized.

All purchases and sales of securities must and are to be made through a registered securities broker or dealer of your choosing with whom you have a contractual relationship and have agreed to accept such broker's or dealer's terms and conditions.

About the Author

Christopher Uhl, a dynamic force in the world of finance, stands as a distinguished personality with a trailblazing career in stock and option trading. Recognized as a two-time Top 100 Person in Finance and the Host of the Top 10 iTunes Investing Podcast, *The How To Trade Stocks And Options Podcast*, Christopher has cultivated a massive following, reaching over 2 million downloads in more than 150 countries.

Christopher's journey to success wasn't without challenges; having faced setbacks, he embarked on a transformative path. Learning directly from World Famous Market Wizards and Billionaire Portfolio Managers, he distilled their teachings into the groundbreaking "10 Minutes To Freedom Trading Strategy." In its inaugural year, this strategy yielded an impressive return of 172.41% in 2021, solidifying Christopher's status as a trailblazer in the realm of trading.

Hailing from humble beginnings in rural Texas, Christopher's pursuit of knowledge led him to earn a BBA and MBA from Henderson State University in Arkadelphia, Arkansas. Despite entering the corporate finance arena during the tumultuous economic landscape of 2008, he navigated the challenges, becoming a Certified Management Accountant all while honing his trading expertise over a decade-long trading career.

This visionary and award-winning personality continues to share his wisdom, aiming to make trading knowledge as accessible as entertainment. Christopher Uhl is not just a trader; he is a mentor, speaker, and innovator, dedicated to empowering traders of all levels with the tools and insights to trade faster and smarter.

His success starting from humble beginnings proves that anyone with a passion of the markets can also find tremendous rewards with enough dedication and perseverance.

By the way, have you subscribed to the How to Trade Stocks and Options Podcast?

It is where we give you specific tools, tips & tricks to trade faster and trade smarter.

If you've been struggling, overwhelmed, and don't know how to start trading, then you need this free podcast! Among other things, it reveals the exact strategies a top 100 person in finance uses to trade, as well as provides interviews from successful traders all over the world, so you can have the tools, tips & tricks to trade faster and trade smarter.

Just go to your favorite podcast platform and type in "How to Trade Stocks and Options Podcast" so you can start listening instantly for free!

There's no catch. I'm doing this because finance and trading are my passion, and I want to help you be successful.

New episodes are released every week. Don't wait! The next one could give you your big breakthrough, and finally, you'll find the success you always dreamed of with trading.

You can even be a part of the show! Just send me a message on social media at @10minutetrading on Twitter and Instagram, and we can add your question to one of our future episodes!

So just to recap, you get instant access to this incredibly valuable free podcast, The "How to Trade Stocks and Options Podcast," that will help give you the tools, tips & tricks to trade faster and trade smarter (including the exact strategies a top 100 person in finance uses to trade as well as interviews from successful traders all over the world)... which means you can finally stop struggling, feeling overwhelmed and not knowing how to start trading.

Just subscribe and start listening today! (Today's episode just might be the one that changes your financial future...)

Chapter 1

The Triple Stock Profit System

The Easy Method to Potentially Triple Profits Just from Owning a Stock

Foreword

What you're holding, "The Triple Stock Profit System" is going to help you specifically with how to utilize the strategic advantages of options trading to make monthly income in addition to owning shares of stock.

I've spent over a decade of my life learning how to trade stocks and options. I want to share with you some of the best lessons I have learned along the way. I made a lot of mistakes and paid a hefty amount of "trader tuition" and I hope this guide will help you on your trading journey by learning from my success and avoiding making the same mistakes I did.

Thank you so much for reading this chapter!

Christopher M. Uhl, CMA

Introduction

In this guide, you'll find a very simple method that can take an ordinary stock trade and give it potentially three avenues to profit.

This isn't any kind of rocket science and it is surprisingly simple. This is a strategy many advanced investors use month after month to generate income.

Think of this strategy like owning rental property. You own the asset, in this case the stock, and every month you make an income just from owning the asset. It's super simple and most average investors have no idea how easy it is to add to their own portfolio.

How to Make Triple Profits on

Any Dividend Yielding Stock

This strategy can be applied to *any dividend yielding stock*. GM was used as an example as it is just about to go ex-dividend at the time of publication, meaning that the shareholders on that date will be recorded and paid the dividend when it is released in the next few weeks.

GM has had a recent bit of publicity lately and anytime a stock is in the news, that means it is more in play with both institutional and retail traders.

Figure 1:

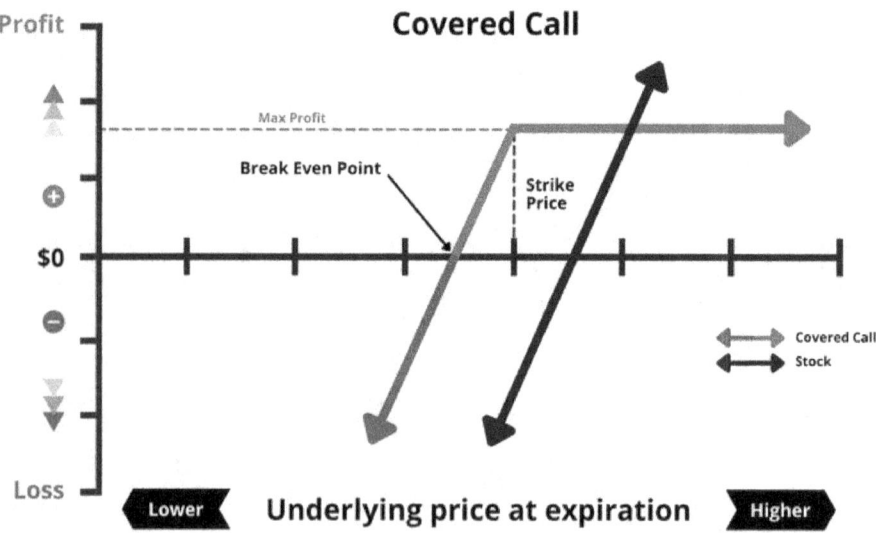

It is apparent that there is an opportunity to profit in several ways on the stock. First, the ex-dividend date is December 6, and with earnings not until February (which could lead to additional volatility), this seems like an ideal candidate for a covered call.

The ex-dividend date is the date upon which the holders of the shares of stock are recorded to receive the dividend, which is paid out a few weeks later.

One would only need to hold the shares on that date to receive the dividend payout. The extrinsic value of the in-the-money puts shows a careful reader of the options chain that there will be an approximately 86-cent dividend per share, or a 2.34 percent return on the current price of $36.69.

By buying the shares, we can expect to see a 2.34% dividend return on this part of the portfolio, which on its own isn't too shabby (certainly better than the vast majority of CD or savings accounts), but we can potentially do even better...

If one were to purchase 100 shares of GM, then an out-of-the-money call could be sold against those shares.

I described in my covered calls guide how these work; you can skip ahead to that chapter to understand this concept fully.

Essentially, we would get to keep the amount of the premium sold on the call plus any gains in the price of the stock, up to the strike price of the call that was sold, and now with the ex-dividend date in the next week, we would get to keep the dividend per share as well!

Buying 100 shares at the price of this writing at $36.69 would cost half the stated amount if buying on margin at $1,834.50.

Then, by selling the January 39 Call at 80 cents per share and taking in the dividend at 86 cents per share for a total of $1.66 per share, you would get a 9 percent return on capital.

If GM goes up to or above $39 per share between now and the January 18, expiration of the call, the trade will make an additional $2.31 per share for a total return of $3.97 per share or a 21.6 percent return on capital in the next 51 days.

Here's the best part: because of taking in the credit on the sale of the call plus the dividend, the breakeven price per share would be $35.03, nearly 5 percent below the current price of $36.69.

With the options having extra premium at this time and the ex-dividend date only a week away, this could potentially be the best time in recent memory to sell a covered call in GM.

By taking this example, you can apply this to any dividend-yielding stock.

1. Buy 100 shares
2. Sell an out-of-the-money call option
3. Collect the dividend

Your profit on the trade comes from 3 different avenues

1. The increase in the share value (assuming it goes up)
2. The premium collected on the call option
3. The dividend

It sounds much more complicated than it truly is, and once you understand the concept of selling covered calls, you're just adding in additional income by selling the calls on dividend-yielding stocks.

Conclusion

This strategy couldn't be simpler. First, buy 100 shares of a dividend yielding stock before the ex-dividend date.

Sell a call against those shares.

Receive the dividend, plus the credit from the call plus any capital appreciation of the stock. There is zero additional risk to selling the call and taking the dividend. The capital appreciation is just icing on the cake at this point!

Chapter 2

The Definitive Guide to Covered Calls

A High Class Problem
that Can Potentially
Guarantee Gains!

Foreword

Covered calls are honestly the very first strategy I encourage new options traders to implement.

It is just so easy.

Just buy 100 shares of stock in your favorite company. Now sell one out of the money call. Look at you, you're an options trader now and you just created a monthly income source that requires no additional risk.

Personally, I feel that owning stock without selling calls against those shares is leaving good money on the table.

Christopher M. Uhl, CMA

Introduction

In this guide, we will cover how to put on a covered call, why you might want to consider adding these to your portfolio in the future, and explain how they can be profitable.

Many people do not understand that if a call goes into the money and is called away, leaving you with no more shares, it's the best outcome! This guide will show why that is and how having shares called away in this manner is the best high-class problem anyone could ask for.

Covered Calls: A High-Class Problem

Do you want to know the greatest high-class problem? Having your covered call go into the money. A covered call is a way to take a long stock trade and give it some extra juice by selling an out-of-the-money call.

Let's say, for example, you really feel strongly that oil is going up. The way you might want to trade that is by buying an oil ETF like USO.

USO's closing price on 5/31/18 was $13.55, making it quite an affordable security to buy. 100 shares of USO would only cost $1,355, and if the broker lets you trade on margin, you may even be able to buy 100 shares for half of that.

Depending on the broker, you can buy a stock for half of its stated price if on margin. And as long as you have enough cash to cover the full value of the stock in your portfolio, you shouldn't have to pay any margin fees for that privilege. Now, this does depend on your broker, but I'm speaking in general terms.

But be warned, if the price of the stock you've bought goes down enough, your broker could issue you a margin call, where you've got to provide additional cash to make the trade.

However, with my experience when I've received margin calls, the easiest option is to just close the trade and take the loss. Sometimes you're wrong, and it's a lot easier to exit a trade and take the loss than find a few extra thousand dollars to wire to your broker.

So you're now long oil, congratulations! I'm sure that Exxon will be very excited. You believe the price of oil will rise, but what if it doesn't?

What if USO goes down 1% to $13.41? Or maybe oil tanks like it did in late May 2018 and dropped 2.5%, down to $13.21? And just like how oil and water don't mix, you decide that you're ready to cut your losses before they become a murky oil slick in your account.

If you had sold a July 14 Call against your 100 shares of stock, your breakeven would actually be at $13.21. Your account wouldn't have any losses at all!

In fact, by selling the call against your long stock, you actually increase the probability of profit from 50%. The $14 Call has a Delta of 34, which means it has approximately a 34% probability of expiring in the money.

If you're familiar with covered calls, I can hear the objection you're thinking already,

"You're limiting my upside, why do I want to do that?"

This is 100% true; a covered call does limit the upside appreciation in the trade, but to me, this actually works in our favor.

By selling the call, we are taking in an immediate credit of 34 cents per share, which offsets the current share price by that amount and explains why our breakeven is lower than the current price.

But we get to keep that 34 cents per share plus the appreciation between the current price of $13.55 and the strike price of $14.00 or 45 cents per share.

The total gain if USO goes to or above $14.00 at expiration would be $34 + $45 for a total profit of $79 on 100 shares of stock.

The shares would be called away by the buyer of the call, but in the meantime, we could have made a return of 5.8% (if we paid the full $1,355 for the shares) or even as much as an 11.7% return on capital if we bought the shares on margin.

Only once USO reaches $14.34 would this trade actually have benefitted by <u>not</u> selling the Call. However, the probability of that happening is even less than the 34% probability of reaching $14.00.

If USO never goes over $14.00, and there's a 66% probability it will not, we still get to keep the $34 we received upfront and can roll the Call out to another month, taking in even more credit, reducing the cost of the shares, and further increasing our probability of profit.

Covered Calls are one of the most basic and easiest options trades to make. They have a higher probability of profit and actually decrease the risk to your account rather than buying shares outright.

Having one go in the money and having the shares called away—that's my kind of high-class problem.

Figure 1.

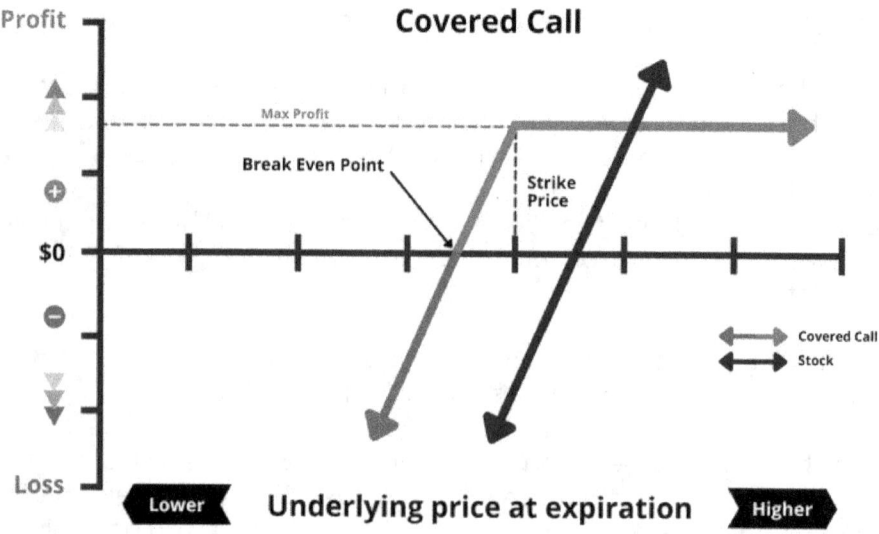

Conclusion

If you own shares of stock, it is advantageous to sell out-of-the-money calls against those shares.

The seller of the call takes in an immediate credit to their account. This credit can be applied to the share's price to reduce the breakeven point.

If the stock does not move at all, the seller keeps all the credit from the call. If the stock goes down, the seller has less risk because the credit taken in has reduced the price per share by the amount of credit.

If the stock goes up, as long as it stays below the Call strike, there is nothing to be done. The owner of the shares takes advantage of the capital appreciation with the rise in share price. They also take advantage of the credit from the sale of the Call.

If it goes into the money, the seller has received the FULL PROFIT that could have been made on the trade. The full profit can be calculated as:

The price of the shares when sold
- The price of the shares when bought
+ The credit received Total Dollar Return

If you are selling the call, the most advantageous call strike to sell is generally the 30 Delta Call. This gives an approximate 70% probability that the price of the stock will be in the money at expiration and called away.

However, that means that 30% of the time it is not called away, leaving the opportunity to sell calls month after month, reducing the breakeven price of the shares with each sale.

Chapter 3

The Definitive Guide to The Options Chain

Discover The Potential Fortune That Lies Hidden In Your Options Chain

Foreword

The options chain is where everything starts. There I was, learning about options trading, overwhelmed and excited with everything there was to learn.

The thing is, at the time, I was staring at a screen full of numbers and thinking to myself, "What on Earth is an iron condor?"

The big problem was I just wanted to make money, so what do all these numbers mean? I realized I would have to dedicate hundreds or even thousands of hours to studying trading because I had no idea how to use the options chain.

Then, as if by chance, something amazing happened...

I realized everything with options was just a combination of only four choices of buying and selling calls and puts. Trading options really wasn't that hard once you knew what you were doing!

Instantly, it became crystal clear to me how I could visually see what the trade would look like based on what the trade cost, and through that, I saw I had a chance to change mine and my family's financial future.

My goal for this chapter is to help you reach your own epiphany with the options chain and to help set you on your own path to financial independence.

Christopher M. Uhl, CMA

Introduction

Richard Branson has a quote that says, "You don't learn to walk by following the rules. You learn by doing and falling over."

Now, being able to trade is going to take some time. As soon as you think you've got it figured out, the market is going to come around and humble you just to keep you in your place.

I've been there. I've had a month where I won every single trade. Then, a month or two later, my accounts went down 25%. Now, I'm wondering, "What is going on?" That's the deal with trading.

You're going to fall, but it's whether you decide to persevere or quit that'll determine your level of success.

Now, you've got to let every losing trade be an opportunity to learn and add those lessons to your skill sets. Please, don't be discouraged. You can do it. That's why you're here, trying to improve your trading talents. It's a lifelong process you're going to either learn to love or love to hate. For me personally, I couldn't imagine doing anything else.

Options Chain Basics

Now, what you see here in Figure 1 is an options chain. This is a screenshot straight from Tastyworks.

Figure 1

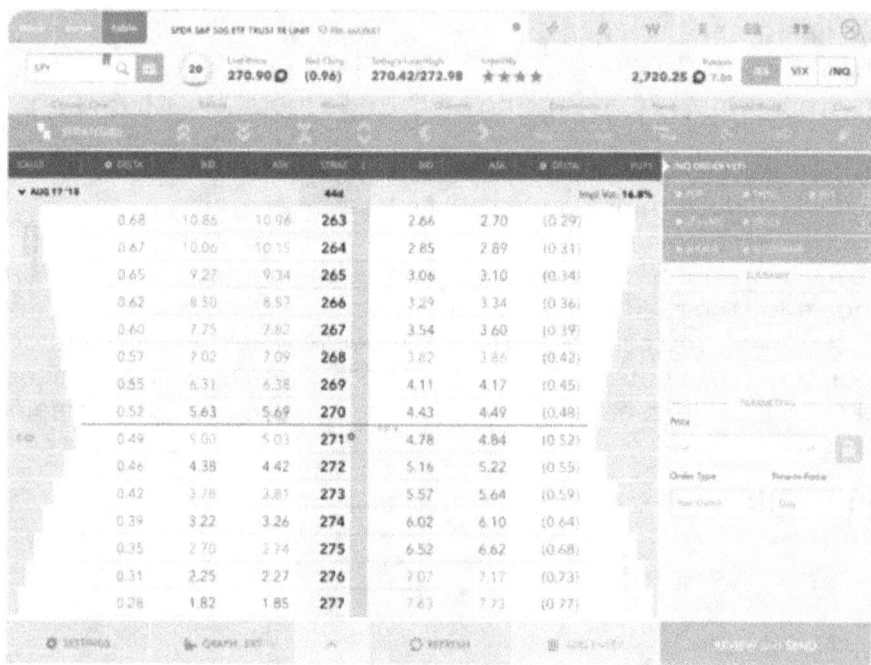

This was taken on July 4th, 2018. This is the screen where you're going to build all your trades.

Now, there's a lot on here. I remember the first time I ever looked at an options chain, and you may be having the same thought right now. What on Earth are all these numbers?

My boss at the time and another colleague were discussing some news in Deutsche Bank. I didn't remember what it was, but he said to the colleague of mine, "Hey, if you really think it's going to go down, you should go out and buy a put."

I remembered hearing about puts in business school, but I couldn't remember anything about them. So, of course, I googled "what is a put?" to see what it was. I learned that I could profit if the stock drops in price. I was like... All right, let me check this out. Little by little, I got hooked.

Then, I opened an option chain just like this one, and I thought, "What on earth is all of this? You've got to be kidding me! I don't even know where to start. I just want to make some money!" So, I totally empathize with what you're probably thinking right now. So today, I'm going to break down each section.

Stock/ETF Information

We will be reviewing the options chain for the SPY (SPDR S&P 500 ETF) in Figure 2 below and this is for August 2018. Now, we're going to start from the top and work our way down left or right.

Figure 2

At the top, you'll see the underlying security. Whether it's a stock, ETF or whatever, it'll all be in the same place.

Next, you'll see the options pricing shown by the IV rank number (where the circle is). On a scale of 1 to 100, when it's one hundred, the circle shown will be full. That means the options are at their highest price of last year. At fifty, it means they're half as high. At zero, it means pretty much any other day of the year the option price is going to be higher. Knowing how to use this to your advantage is going to be a huge help when you make an options trade.

Next, this is the stock price, today's change, and the highs and lows for the day. Then the final metric across the top is a liquidity indicator.

It is vital that you have liquidity. I can't stress this enough. Without liquidity, you're not going to be able to get in or out of a trade. You're not going to be able to get it for the right price you're looking for, and you certainly will have a chance that a profitable trade will turn unprofitable. Then you're going to be stuck in it because nobody wants to take the other side of that trade.

Expiration

Now what you see here in Figure 3 is the top bar, the options chain, and the options expiration cycle.

Figure 3

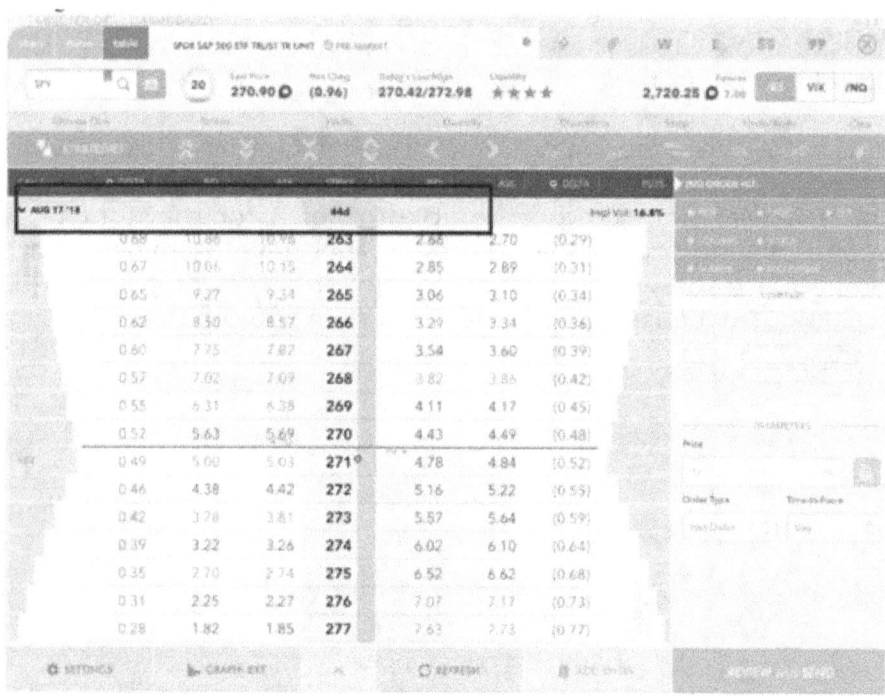

At this point, when it crosses August 17, 2018, all the options that are in the money will be exercised. All the options out of the money will be worthless. So, you want to make sure (if you're buying an option) it stays in the money at that point in time.

Now, you can change this to any time from now for the next couple of years. Each expiration has its own options chain.

It's rare to have an option exercised by the buyer of the option before expiration unless an event comes up like a dividend being paid.

In the Money & Out of the Money

Now, each one of these shaded areas in Figure 4 is in the money.

Figure 4

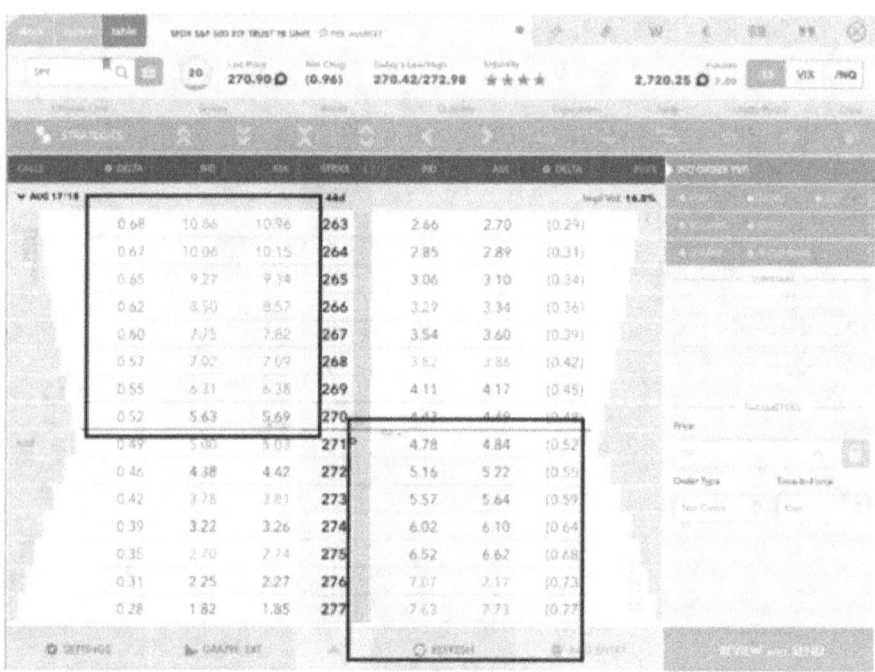

It's denoted by the strikes (where the shading is a little bit grayish yellow there). If the strike is in the money at expiration, it will be automatically exercised by your broker. You do not have to do anything. It just means you will own (if you're long a call) one hundred shares of stock in your account the following morning.

Now, you can see that the shading in Figure 4 changes from top to bottom and left to right. That's because there's the call side which is the left side, then the puts which are on the right side, and being in the money is different on either side.

This line in the middle of Figure 5 is the "at the money" spot where you can see how the 270 is on the left-hand side is shaded. The 271s are not. That's the delineator here to say what is and isn't in the money; because the stock price is currently at $270.90.

Figure 5

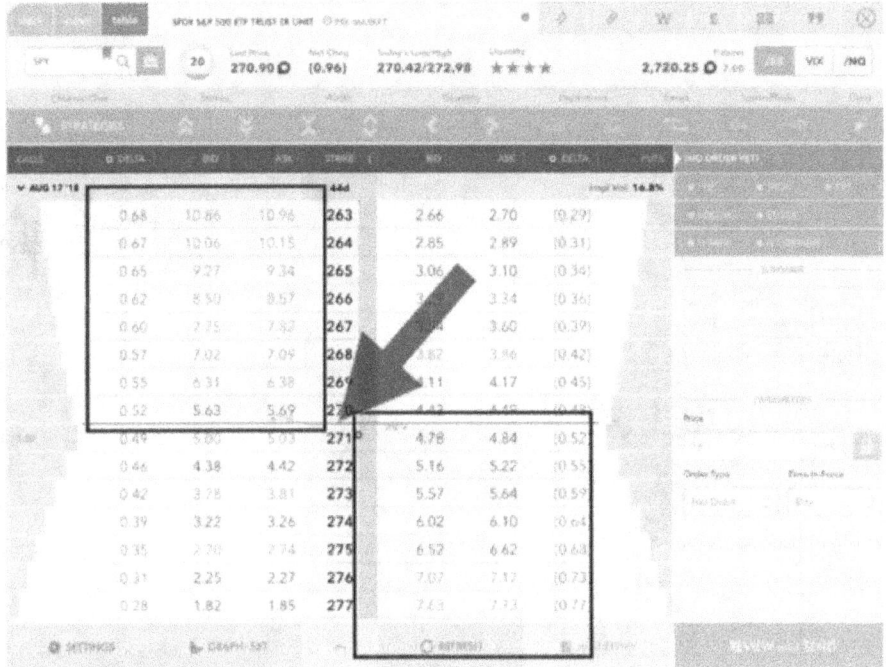

Selling a Call Option

Calls increase in value as the underlying stock price moves up. When you buy a call option, you're wanting the price of the underlying stock to go up. When you sell a call option, you want the underlying price to go down.

To sell a call, you're going to click the number under the "bid" heading as shown in Figure 6.

Figure 6

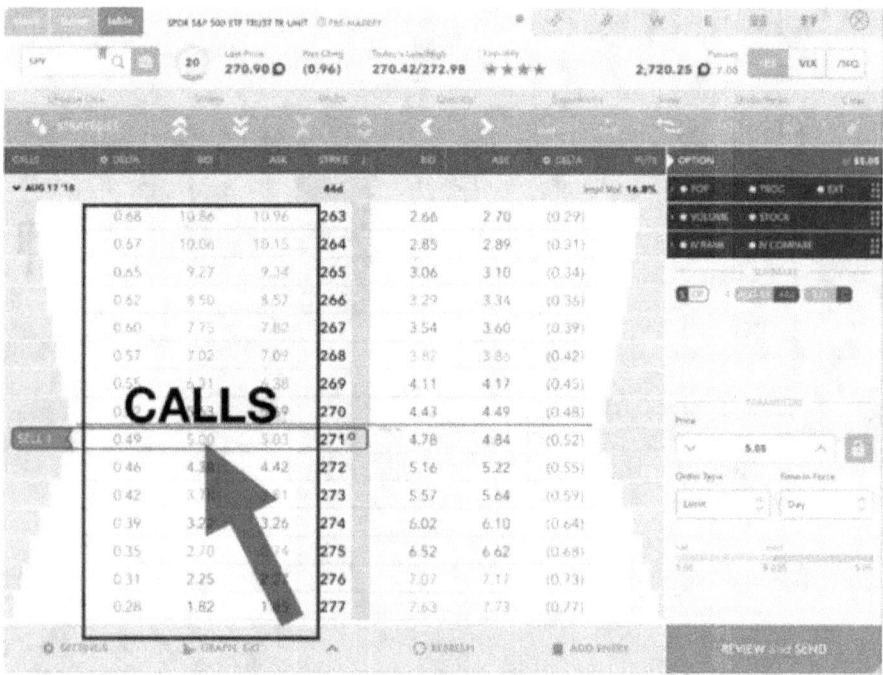

You're going to put it up for bids to sell the contract. Now, the strike is going to light up red when you sell a call. When selling a call, you ideally want it to stay out of the money. Otherwise, you're going to have to pay the buyer the difference of the strike price and the stock price at expiration, which could be unprofitable to you as the seller.

Buying a Call Option

Now if one is looking to buy a call, they're going to click the number under the "ask" column shown in Figure 7.

Figure 7

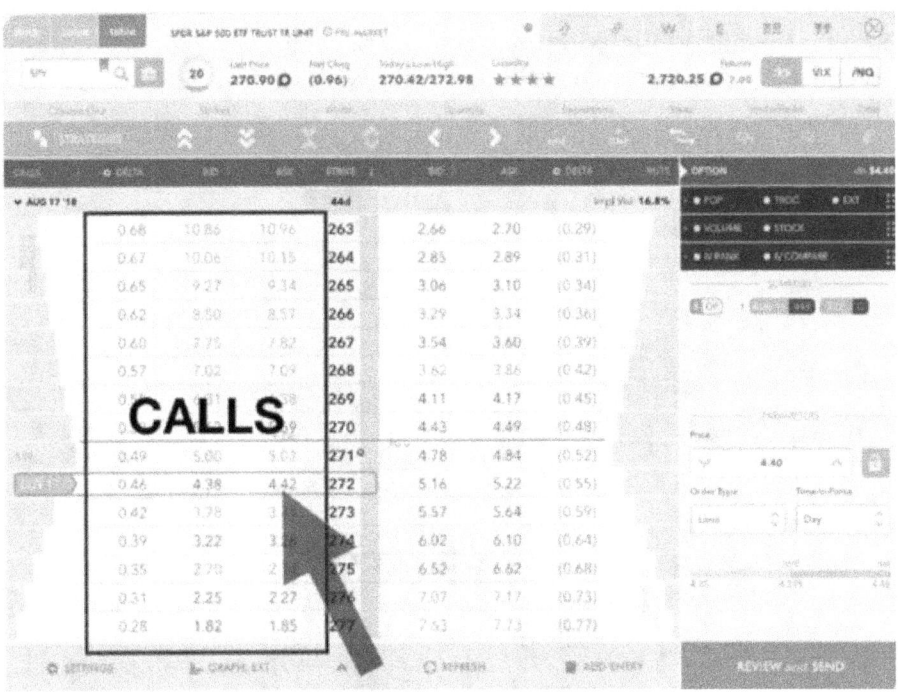

And just like that, it's going to light up green. Now, there are only two things you can do with a call - buy it or sell it. All the trades we make are a combination of buying and selling to achieve various setups and profit targets.

Buying a Put Option

Puts are the opposite of calls, allowing you to buy, sell, or create a combination. Puts increase in value as the underlying stock price moves down. When you buy a put option, you want the price of the underlying stock to go down. When you sell a put option, you want the underlying stock price to go up.

Similar to calls, when you buy a put, you'll click the "ask" value under the "ask" button shown in Figure 8. It will light up green, just like that.

Figure 8

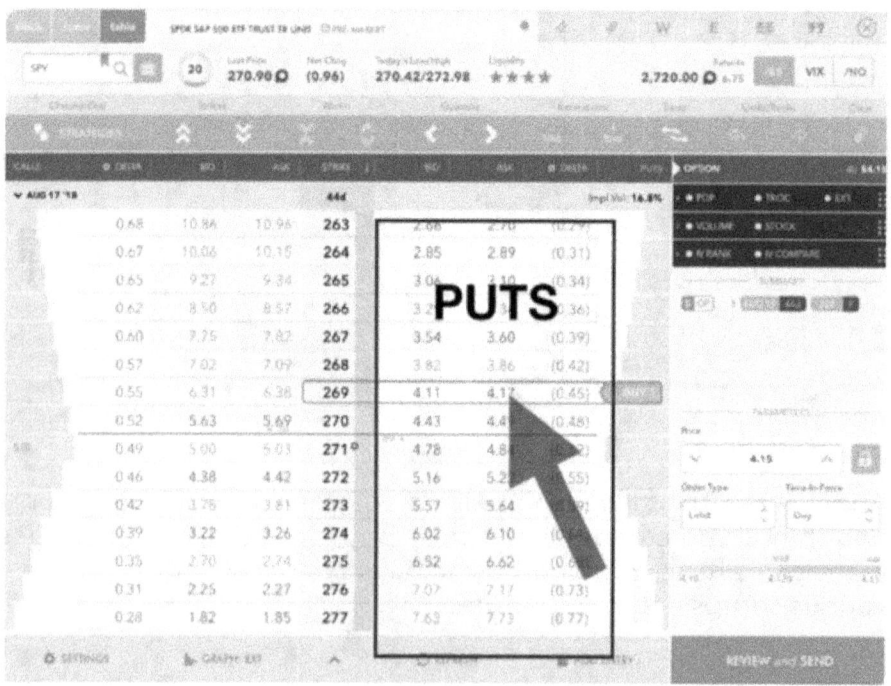

Selling a Put Option

When you sell a put, you're going to click one under the "bid" column, just like shown in Figure 9, it's going to light up red.

Figure 9

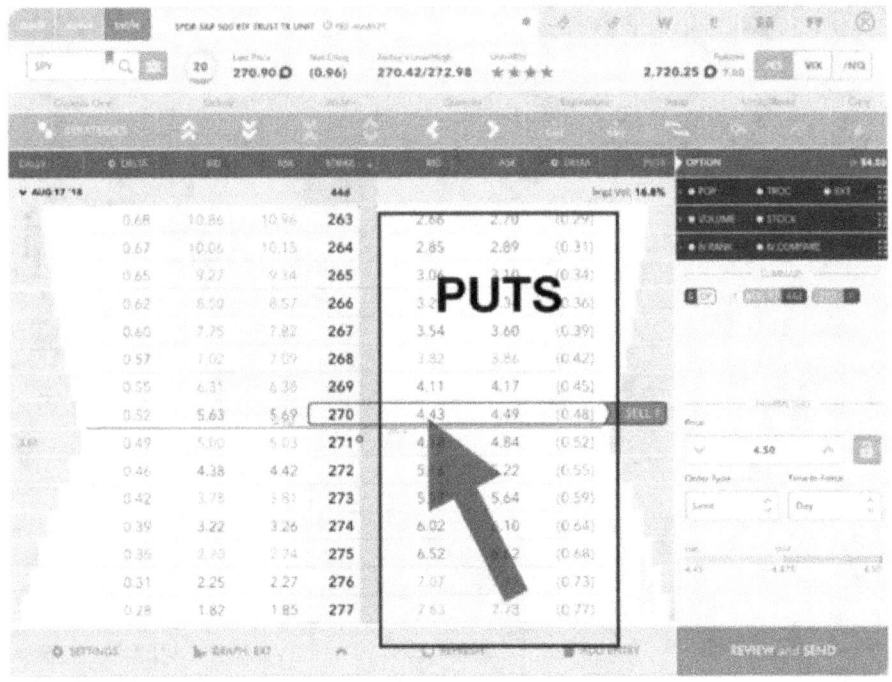

Combining Options

Now, you can add up to four legs in a single trade as shown in Figure 10 and it can be various amounts of quantities.

Figure 10

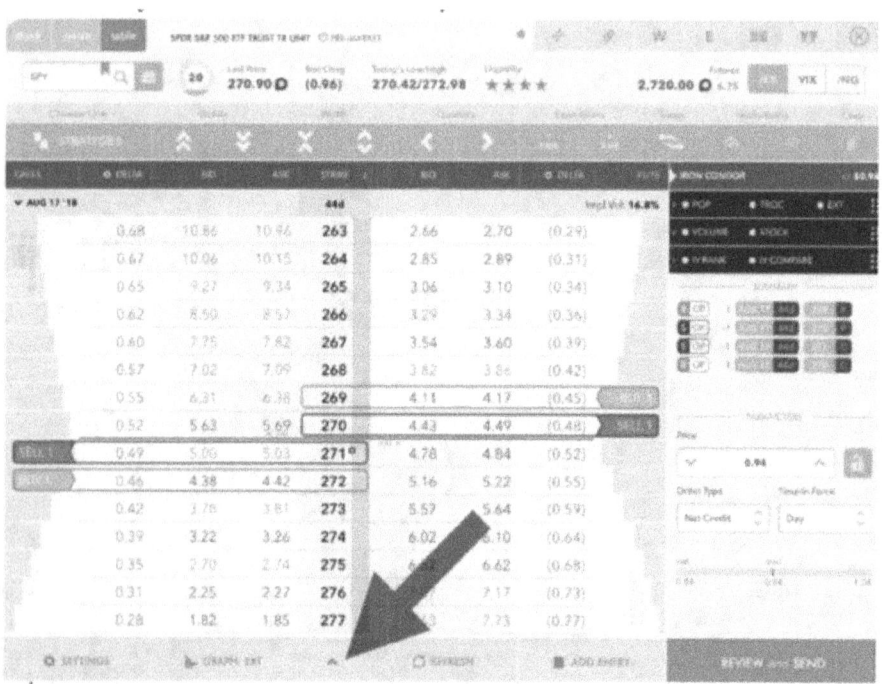

You may have two short calls (meaning that you've sold them) and three long puts (meaning that you've bought them). The quantity of each strike doesn't matter; it's just the number of strikes you've chosen that is limited to four.

After you've got all your orders set up here, you can click the little arrow down at the bottom, also shown in Figure 10, which will reveal the information shown in Figure 11.

Decoding the Information Behind the Numbers

Figure 11 shows all the trade information that is hiding behind the numbers in your options chain.

Figure 11

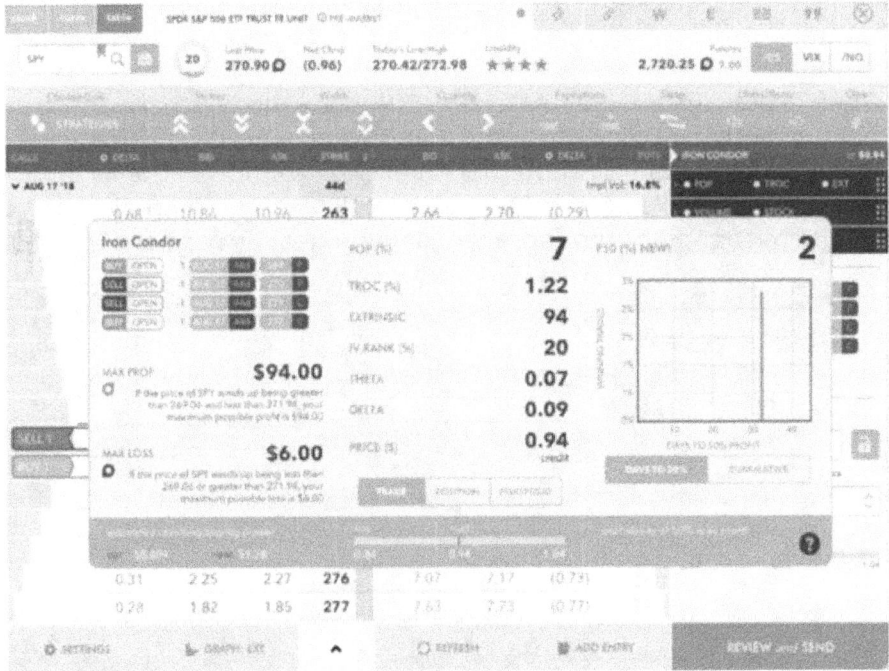

It's going to show you your max profit, your max loss, your probability of profit, and your Greeks (such as Delta and Theta).

Greeks are variables assigned to represent different characteristics of an option. We spend more time dissecting their meaning in a later chapter.

It'll also show your account value - this is an $8 account I created for demonstration purposes. It's going to show you your buying power, what you currently have, and what's left over.

After you place this trade, you can see that the max profit in this trade is $94. That's great, but it has a 7% chance of that actually happening just based on the setup here. What's your max loss? Hey! That's only six dollars. So, it's a tiny risk, and it's a very tiny chance it'll actually pay off.

There are a ton of numbers here, and I know it can be really confusing at the start. But with practice, it just becomes second nature.

When I pull up an options chain, I know exactly where to go to make exactly the kind of trade that I want, and I'm not really too concerned about finding the bid, the ask, or whatever the case may be. I just know exactly where I need to click, and I'm confident you will get to that point the more familiar you get with options trading.

Intrinsic and Extrinsic Value
of Options

With options, there are two kinds of value. There are intrinsic values and extrinsic values.

So, let's take a look at the header in Figure 12.

Figure 12

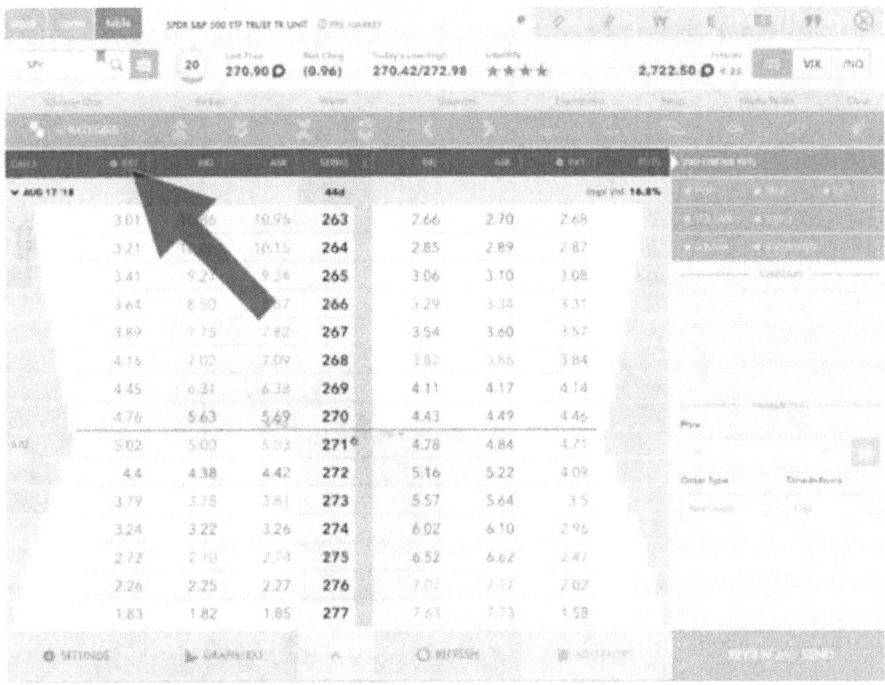

You can click this section here to reveal all kinds of information. If you look back at all previous figures, you'll see that this section of the header showed the Delta value. Now, we have changed it to show the extrinsic value of the options.

All the options you see on this page have extrinsic value. When you sell options, you're looking to sell the highest value and watch it expire to zero. Extrinsic value means the amount of money that the option is worth is above the difference in the stock price and the strike price.

Now, beyond extrinsic value, we have intrinsic value. When a stock goes in the money, it gains intrinsic value. Intrinsic value is the amount of the stock price minus the strike price. All of the options have extrinsic value, but only the options that are in the money have intrinsic value.

Figure 13

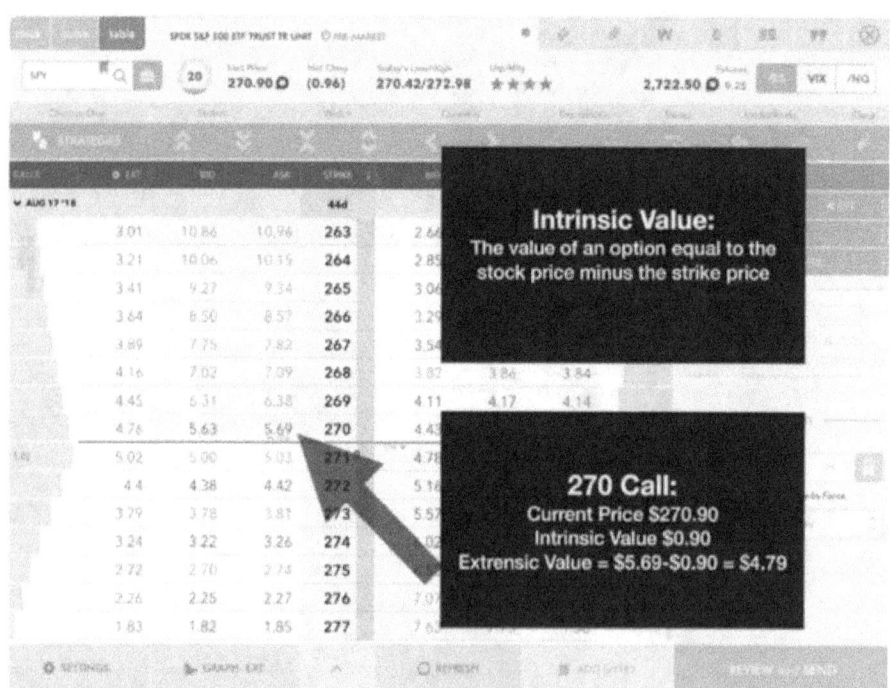

Figure 13 is shown here with the strike of 271, and the stock is at $270.90. It's not in the money because the stock is below 271.

If it expired right now, this option is worthless because it expired out of the money. This option currently, if you were to buy it, would be $5.03. So, $503.00 (because the price shown is per share and options are grouped in lots of 100 shares per contract) would be coming out of your account to buy it.

That's pure extrinsic value because the call is out of the money, but it's closer to being in the money than 272 (which is at $4.42 if you were to buy it).

It has a higher chance of being in the money, which is why it has a higher price associated with it. As you can see from the left-hand sidebar, all of the options here have extrinsic value.

Extrinsic value can be based on time expected moves, implied volatility, or a combination of all those: the less time - the less extrinsic value, the less implied volatility - the less extrinsic value, the smaller expected move - the smaller extrinsic value.

You can see the difference here; the 270 call is worth $5.69, or the 263 call at the top line here is at $10.96. That's because it's in the money by $7.00.

The deeper in the money the option is, the more intrinsic value grows. The intrinsic value will move cent for cent with the stock price. So, if the current price is at $270.90 (like in Figure 13), the intrinsic value of the 270 call is 90 cents.

The extrinsic value is $4.76. That's shown on the far left. You can calculate that by taking $5.69, which is the current stock price minus ninety cents (an intrinsic value), and you get $4.79, with $4.76 being the midpoint between $5.63 and $5.69.

Now, if the overall goal for an option seller is to have the option expire worthless because it's out of the money, an option buyer wants the stock to go as deep into the money as possible to gain the most intrinsic and extrinsic value.

Changes in Value

One thing to notice in Figure 14 is the further away from the money strikes, the prices of the options and the extrinsic value goes down.

Figure 14

If these options were to expire right here, they would be worth zero to the option buyer, who would lose the full premium they paid, yet they would be at full profit to the option seller who is keeping the full premium paid by the buyer.

In reality, when we sell out of the money options, we want to be junk sellers. We want to take these financial instruments that could possibly be worth nothing and find a buyer.

We just wait for it to go down in price, then what we sold we can buy back for a lesser price and keep the difference.

Skew

There's another pricing variable called skew. Skew shows which direction there is more risk for the trade. If we go five dollars away on either side, you'll see that the calls are worth less than the puts for the same distance, as shown in Figure 14.

So, if we're saying 271 is at the money, we're going to go $5 its way to 276. You'll see that if you were to buy a call, and it's at $2.27, or if you were to buy a put, it's at $3.34. So, it's over $1.00 difference for five dollars away from the current price. What this shows here is the market is placing a higher premium on it going down than it going up.

Conclusion

This is the framework from which all options trades are born. Everything to put on an options trade is going to be done on the type of screens shown throughout this guide.

You've got to get to know these options chains. I would suggest that you open and check out a ton of them to see what they look like. Everyone is going to be a little different. They're going to have differing strike widths and differing expiration terms; some will be expensive and some will be relatively cheap.

With this guide, you now have the framework to know where to click and what each section means. With practice, experience, and a few expensive lessons, I'm confident that you will develop your own set of skills to become a successful options trader too!

Chapter 4

**The Definitive Guide to Easy
Options Greeks**

Very Soon it Won't Be All Greek to You!

Foreword

There are many components to create the Black-Scholes Options Pricing Model, and we could have an entire encyclopedia on the different intricacies of that model and all its inputs.

But why?

In this chapter, we are going to focus on what matters to you and your portfolio. The Options Pricing Greeks are important, without a doubt, but how can you actually use them in practice versus plugging them into a model?

Once you master how to read and use the Greeks, you'll find they become second nature. You'll know at a glance so much more about your portfolio than the average investor, and you will know where things are going right and going wrong potentially before it shows up on your bottom line.

One of the things that scare most people away from trading options is the potentially significant learning curve. I'm here to help with that and to explain the options to Greeks as easily as I possibly can.

Christopher M. Uhl, CMA

Introduction

We will be covering many of the Greeks in this guide, but this is not a comprehensive list. There are first, second, third, and fourth derivatives to these options pricing components.

This guide is meant to serve you and give you the necessary information to enact action without being overwhelmed by data.

What is an option's Greek?

Option Greeks are all the pieces that go into the options price and when utilized correctly can help a trader be more effective at managing risk. There's Delta, Theta, Vega, Beta, Alpha, Gamma, and Rho, and more...

It sounds scary and intimidating, but you know what, it really doesn't matter what goes into the Black Scholes option pricing model. (I bet you didn't think you'd be reading that today...) Honestly, I do not give any time, attention, or care whatsoever to the Black Scholes option pricing model because the theory behind the options price really doesn't matter to the trader.

What really matters is: what does it mean to you, what are the prices actually telling you today, and how can we use this information to potentially increase returns and reduce risk?

Delta

First, we are going to be taking a look at the option's Delta, what it means to you, and how it works in your own portfolio. I'm going to explain it as easily as I possibly can because topics like the Greeks usually scare people away from trading options, and that's what I don't want.

I want to give you everything I know so you can apply this in your own portfolio and hopefully take better trading actions now that you're armed with this information.

So when we're talking about options, the first thing I look at whenever I'm looking at the Greeks, is Delta.

I mean it.

That's really the number one go-to options Greek that I look at is Delta. I'm going to give you three reasons why I consider it to be the very most important of all the options Greeks.

The textbook definition of Delta is "The price change of the option for every $1 move in the underlying stock price."

Now, what does that mean to you? Calls have Deltas going from zero to one; puts have them from zero to negative one. For the context of this, we're going to be assuming that zero is still zero and one being one hundred. Traders generally talk about 20 Delta, 50 Delta, or 75 Delta, whatever the case may be, they're taking off the decimal instead of saying 0.20 Delta, 0.50 Delta, or 0.75 Delta.

So let's look at an options chain, and I'll give you some real-world examples of how we can use Delta.

Figure 1:

CALLS	Ø DELTA	BID	ASK	STRIKE	BID	ASK	Ø DELTA	PUTS
⌄ FEB 15 '19				46d				Impl Vol. 12.6%
	0.89	6.80	7.55	114	0.16	0.29	(0.10)	
	0.87	6.25	6.55	115	0.24	0.34	(0.13)	
	0.83	5.35	5.65	116	0.38	0.43	(0.17)	
	0.78	4.50	4.80	117	0.54	0.61	(0.22)	
	0.72	3.75	4.00	118	0.74	0.83	(0.28)	
	0.65	3.00	3.20	119	1.05	1.11	(0.36)	
	0.56	2.42	2.56	120	1.40	1.55	(0.44)	
	0.48	1.90	2.03	121	1.89	2.05	(0.52)	1.97
	0.40	1.49	1.59	122	2.42	2.74	(0.59)	
	0.33	1.10	1.23	123	3.10	3.35	(0.66)	
	0.27	0.83	0.95	124	3.80	4.15	(0.72)	
	0.21	0.61	0.74	125	4.55	4.95	(0.76)	
	0.17	0.51	0.57	126	5.40	6.05	(0.79)	
	0.13	0.33	0.44	127	6.30	6.90	(0.82)	
	0.11	0.29	0.35	128	7.30	7.90	(0.84)	

Ok, so what we're looking at here in Figure 1 is the options chain for TLT in February 2018, and TLT has a 48 percent implied volatility rank as shown in the circle near the top.

That means option prices are pretty high right now. Now, let us talk about Delta. The circled area on the left in Figure 2 is the Delta for the calls and on the right is the Delta for the puts.

As you can see, like I talked about a minute ago, put Deltas are negative, and call Deltas are positive.

Figure 2:

So going back to the textbook definition of Delta. If we were to look at the 119 put as circled in Figure 3, that has a 36 Delta. A 36 Delta means that on the put side, it is referring to if the price of TLT went down by a dollar in value as the underlying stock price decreases; so it has a negative Delta.

Figure 3:

CALLS	⊙ DELTA	BID	ASK	STRIKE	BID	ASK	⊙ DELTA	PUTS
FEB 15 '19				46d			Impl Vol: 12.6%	
	0.89	6.80	7.55	114	0.16	0.29	(0.10)	
	0.87	6.25	6.55	115	0.24	0.34	(0.13)	
	0.83	5.35	5.65	116	0.38	0.43	(0.17)	
	0.78	4.50	4.80	117	0.54	0.61	(0.22)	
	0.72	3.75	4.00	118	0.74	0.83	(0.26)	
	0.65	3.00	3.20	119	1.05	1.11	(0.36)	
	0.56	2.42	2.56	120	1.40	1.55	(0.44)	
	0.48	1.90	2.03	121	1.89	2.05	(0.52)	
	0.40	1.49	1.59	122	2.42	2.74	(0.59)	
	0.33	1.10	1.23	123	3.10	3.35	(0.66)	
	0.27	0.83	0.95	124	3.80	4.15	(0.72)	
	0.21	0.61	0.74	125	4.55	4.95	(0.76)	
	0.17	0.51	0.57	126	5.40	6.05	(0.79)	
	0.13	0.33	0.44	127	6.30	6.90	(0.82)	
	0.11	0.29	0.35	128	7.20	7.80	(0.84)	

If the price of TLT went down by a dollar from $121.05 to $120.05, this particular option would increase in value by 36 cents, and we get that from the 36 Delta. TLT has to go down by a dollar, and the price of the option will go up by 36 cents. It's not a one-for-one relationship here. It won't ever be unless it's super deep in the money, and the price and the time are about to expire.

So, let's look at the other side of that in Figure 4. Let's look at a 125 call that has a 21 Delta. Now 21 Delta (just like on the put side 21 Delta) means that the price of the option would go up by 21 cents if the price of TLT went up by $1.00.

Figure 4:

TLT			48	Last Price 121.05	Net Chng 0.00	Today's Low/High 0.00/121.05	Liquidity ★★★★			2,506

CALLS	O DELTA	BID	ASK	STRIKE	BID	ASK	O DELTA	PUTS
FEB 15 '19				46d				Impl Vol 12.6%
	0.89	6.80	7.55	114	0.16	0.29	(0.10)	
	0.87	6.25	6.55	115	0.24	0.34	(0.13)	
	0.83	5.35	5.65	116	0.38	0.43	(0.17)	
	0.78	4.50	4.80	117	0.54	0.61	(0.22)	
	0.72	3.75	4.00	118	0.74	0.83	(0.28)	
	0.65	3.00	3.20	119	1.05	1.11	(0.36)	
	0.56	2.42	2.56	120	1.40	1.55	(0.44)	
	0.48	1.90	2.03	121○	1.89	2.05	(0.52)	
	0.40	1.49	1.59	122	2.42	2.74	(0.59)	
	0.33	1.10	1.23	123	3.10	3.35	(0.66)	
	0.27	0.83	0.95		3.80	4.15	(0.72)	
	0.21	0.61	0.74	125	4.55	4.95	(0.76)	
	0.17	0.51	0.57		5.40	6.05	(0.79)	
	0.13	0.33	0.44	127	6.30	6.90	(0.82)	
	0.11	0.28	0.35	128	7.20	7.80	(0.84)	

Being in the money means that it is going to expire and have value or expire and have no value. If it's in the money, it'll expire and have value. The "at-the-money" strike is the strike closest to the current stock price and will be the determinant if the option is in or out of the money at expiration.

If it's out of the money, it expires worthless. If the option moves further into the money or further out of the money, the Delta will show you how much the price of the option will actually change. In the two examples with the 119 put and the 125 call, those would change in price by 36 cents and 21 cents respectively.

Delta can be used to find the probability that the option will expire in the money.

Now if we were to buy a stock, the only way that it profits is if the stock price goes up. If we were to short sell stock, the only way it profits is if it goes down. And with options, we know that we have some flexibility.

We have a higher probability of profit if we're selling out of the money options than if we were to just buy the options outright. So, let's take a look at the TLT options chain again in Figure 5.

Figure 5:

CALLS	Δ DELTA	BID	ASK	STRIKE	BID	ASK	Δ DELTA	PUTS
∨ FEB 15 '19				46d				Impl Vol 12.6%
	0.89	6.80	7.55	114	0.16	0.29	(0.10)	
	0.87	6.25	6.55	115	0.24	0.34	(0.13)	
	0.83	5.35	5.65	116	0.38	0.43	(0.17)	
	0.78	4.50	4.80	117	0.54	0.61	(0.22)	
	0.72	3.75	4.00	118	0.74	0.83	(0.28)	
	0.65	3.00	3.20	119	1.05	1.11	(0.36)	
	0.56	2.42	2.56	120	1.40	1.55	(0.44)	
	0.48	1.90	2.03	121◦	1.89	2.05	(0.52)	
	0.40	1.49	1.59	122	2.42	2.74	(0.59)	
	0.33	1.10	1.23	123	3.10	3.35	(0.66)	
	0.27	0.83	0.95		3.80	4.15	(0.72)	
	0.21	0.61	0.74	125	4.55	4.95	(0.76)	
	0.17	0.51	0.57		5.40	6.05	(0.79)	
	0.13	0.33	0.44	127	6.30	6.90	(0.82)	
	0.11	0.28	0.35	128	7.20	7.80	(0.84)	

TLT 48 Last Price 121.05 | Net Chng 0.00 | Today's Low/High 0.00/121.05 ★★★★ | Liquidity 2,506

We could talk about how we can use the probability of profit shown right here on the screen using Delta. So if we were to look at the 125 call again, it has a Delta of 21, as you remember.

Now that means if someone were to buy that call, it has a 21 percent probability of expiring in-the-money, which is not good. We want to expire the money if we're buying calls; but, if we were to sell the call that means it would be the inverse of that.

If it has a 21 percent chance of expiring in-the-money, it has a 79 percent chance of expiring out of the money.

Figure 6:

So which sounds better to you, 21 percent probability profit or 79 percent probability profit? So to me, that's selling the call and having 79 percent probability profit, and it's shown right there on the screen using Delta.

Now let's say we do the opposite on the put side. Let's say that we are looking at the 119 put again as shown in Figure 6. That has a 36 Delta. So that means the 119 put has a 36 percent probability of expiring in-the-money at expiration. But, it also has a 64 percent chance of expiring out of the money expiration.

So if we were going to choose the two of those which sounds better? Selling something away from the money and having a higher probability of profit than if we were to just buy it outright.

That's why options selling is so powerful because both of these two situations here (both of these two strikes) have a higher than 50/50 probability of profit shown right here on the trade screen by their Delta values.

Then as you look down the chain here as we talked about earlier, the 121 strike is the at-the-money strike where it's probability of profit is roughly 50/50. The further away you go out of the money, the lower the Delta gets which would go hand-in-hand with the probability of profit. Then the further into the money you go, that shows a higher probability of profit it shows a higher Delta because TLT has to move farther to go out of the money in order to not profit. So, for example, the 127 is 6 strikes in the money; and because of that, it has an 82 Delta. So it has an 82 percent probability profit.

Delta represents how much directional exposure you have to the underlying stock price.

So what I mean by that is, if you had one hundred shares of stock, you would have one hundred positive Deltas. It's a static 100 Delta move for every one dollar change in the underlying stock. Remember your option's price would move by one dollar. So in this case, because we're talking about the underlying stock, it's going to move one for one with the options price at 100 Delta.

But we can talk about how we can use the directional exposure associated with those Deltas to give us an idea of how much leverage we have in either direction.

Figure 7:

CALLS	⚙ DELTA	BID	ASK	STRIKE	BID	ASK	⚙ DELTA	PUTS
FEB 15 '19				**46d**			Impl Vol **12.6%**	
	0.89	6.80	7.55	**114**	0.16	0.29	(0.10)	
	0.87	6.25	6.55	**115**	0.24	0.34	(0.13)	
	0.83	5.35	5.65	**116**	0.38	0.43	(0.17)	
	0.78	4.50	4.80	**117**	0.54	0.61	(0.22)	
	0.72	3.75	4.00	**118**	0.74	0.83	(0.28)	
	0.65	3.00	3.20	**119**	1.05	1.11	(0.36)	
		2.42	2.56	**120**	1.40	1.55		
	0.48	1.90	2.03	**121**	1.89	2.05	(0.52)	
		1.49	1.59	**122**	2.42	2.74		
	0.33	1.10	1.23	**123**	3.10	3.35	(0.66)	
	0.27	0.83	0.95	**124**	3.80	4.15	(0.72)	
	0.21	0.61	0.74	**125**	4.55	4.95	(0.76)	
	0.17	0.51	0.57	**126**	5.40	6.05	(0.79)	
	0.13	0.33	0.44	**127**	6.30	6.90	(0.82)	
	0.11	0.38	0.35	**128**	7.50	7.90	(0.84)	

If we look at the 121 call strike in Figure 7, it has a 48 Delta. That means that we would essentially have 48 short shares of stock that we'd be associating with if we sold this call. Our portfolio value would change similarly to owning 48 shares of TLT in our portfolio instead of one call.

Now on the other side of that. Let's look at the 121 put in Figure 7. The 121 put has a 52 Delta. So if we sold the 121 put it would be just like if we bought 52 shares of TLT in our portfolio.

Figure 8:

CALLS	Θ DELTA	BID	ASK	STRIKE	BID	ASK	Θ DELTA	PUTS
	0.89	6.80	7.55	114	0.16	0.29	(0.10)	
	0.87	6.25	6.55	115	0.24	0.34	(0.13)	
	0.83	5.35	5.65	116	0.38	0.43	(0.17)	
	0.78	4.50	4.80	117	0.54	0.61	(0.22)	
	0.72	3.75	4.00	118	0.74	0.83	(0.29)	
	0.65	3.00	3.20	119	1.05	1.11	(0.36)	
	0.56	2.42	2.56	120	1.40	1.55	(0.44)	
	0.48	1.90	2.03	121	1.89	2.05	(0.52)	
	0.40	1.49	1.59	122	2.42	2.74	(0.59)	
	0.33	1.10	1.23	123	3.10	3.35	(0.66)	
	0.27	0.83	0.95	124	3.80	4.15	(0.72)	
	0.21	0.61	0.74	125	4.55	4.95	(0.76)	
	0.17	0.51	0.57	126	5.40	6.05	(0.79)	
	0.13	0.33	0.44	127	6.30	6.90	(0.82)	
	0.11	0.29	0.35	128	7.30	7.90	(0.84)	

That's the way the risk profile would move. Now we could actually work with this a little bit. Looking at Figure 8, let's say that we decided to sell a 125 call with the 21 Delta; then, we decided to sell a 117 put with a 22 Delta. Now those would actually nearly balance off of each other, and you would have most of a zero Delta meaning a neutral trade.

Now a neutral portfolio Delta means that it can go up or down or go nowhere at all. And that's one of the really cool ways to sell options, you don't have to have a bullish or bearish assumption. It can sit right where it's at, between the 117 and the 125, with both of those Delta's nearly balancing off to each other, you've got a very neutral trade that you can put on to potentially profit from TLT not moving at all and trading sideways.

Delta

So, an option's Delta (while it may be the most important Greek in my opinion) can be kind of complicated. But if you take a look at the underlying components of it and know how it's used, it can actually be somewhat simple.

Now the first way to use it is just like the textbook definition. **What is the price change of the option for every $1 change in the underlying stock price?**

The second way to use it is: **What's the probability of this option expiring in-the-money at expiration? What's our probability of profit?**

The third way to look at it is: **What is your directional exposure?** How many shares is this one option representing in your portfolio? Is it at 50 shares? Is it 10 shares?

Delta is the most powerful Greek because *it shows so much information just from one value.* Knowing how to harness this information and use it smartly in your portfolio is key to long term success in trading.

Theta

Now, **Theta** is exactly what you want to have if you're selling options, but exactly what you don't want to have if you're buying options.

Theta is the time value of an option.

All options contracts have a stated expiration date. This is different from stocks because stocks can be held forever, just ask Uncle Warren (Buffet) whereas an option must expire in the money to have a value or if it expires out of the money it is worth zero.

The way that I personally think about it is like an insurance contract. I used to work in the insurance industry. In fact, I've held two jobs in the insurance industry; and if you ever buy a six-month insurance policy, you know without a doubt it's going to cost less than a twelve-month insurance policy.

That's because the insurance company, *aka the options seller,* is keeping in mind **more things can happen over time**. Because of that, they are expecting a higher premium.

Higher premium, just like if you sold an option. Higher premium, if you bought an insurance contract. Do you see how the two are related?

The insurance company is selling its car insurance policy to you for $100. Let's say you crash into an oak tree, you're fine but your Chevrolet Malibu isn't, it's a total loss. The insurance company fulfills their end of the policy by paying you $17,000, meaning they lost $16,900 on the transaction.

This same principle applies to options selling. If I sell a call for $1.00 and it goes $170 into the money, I'm out $16,900 ([$170 in the money - $1 premium collected] x 100 shares). However, I know the risk of that happening is shown by the Delta value as described above and could be very low.

Now we can protect ourselves from catastrophic losses by selling defined risk spreads, which we will cover in a later chapter. Insurance companies have what's called reinsurance, where they buy insurance against large losses from other companies, essentially buying insurance on the insurance they sold, capping their risk.

Now, as you can imagine, a one-month insurance contract would cost less than a two-month insurance contract, two months less than a three-month, three months less than a six-month, and etc. The same holds true for insurance policies and for options contracts.

Now, let's extrapolate that into options pricing. The further you get out in time, the more expensive it is; the closer you get to expiration, the less expensive it is, all things held equal.

That's because of the Theta value. Theta is just like an insurance contract. On day one, it starts at one hundred. On day zero when there's no more time to expire, it's at zero. It will decline from one hundred to zero over the amount of time that the buyer holds the option.

So if you were an option seller, you want to sell the contract when it is costing as much as possible; because you want it to go down. You want Theta and all the other Greeks to be working in your favor.

Now, this really is the enemy of the options buyer, and I've learned firsthand about this.

When I first started trading I lost two thirds of my account in the first 60 days.

I was the guy who was really excited about options. I was buying the mess out of them. **I was buying every option that I could.**

Because of that, I was having time work against me, and I remember just every day watching my account go down and down and down even though the stock was moving in my direction. (Let's say I bought out-of-the-money calls.)

Even though the stock was moving in my direction, the Theta component was larger than the Delta component. The loss of value because of the passage of time was greater than the increase in value due to the underlying stock price move.

In my scenario, it was causing the value of the option to go down; therefore, I as the options buyer was losing money even though it was moving in the direction I wanted.

Now, the curve of the options premium is not linear, it's not a straight line. It actually accelerates, and the prices start to go down faster and faster as it gets closer to the expiration date, but research has shown the best time to be selling premium is around 45 days.

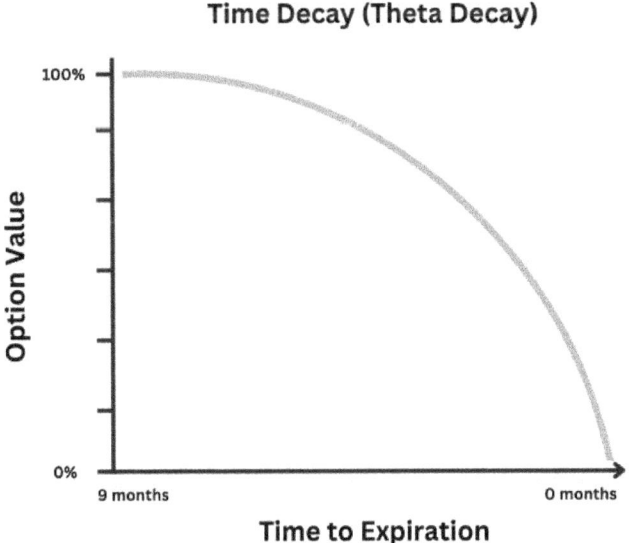

Time Decay (Theta Decay)

That's because it hasn't started the accelerated decline. It hasn't started to take on more risk to the options seller, but it is already starting to show a faster decline than if you were to go out in 90 days or 120 days.

So essentially, if you were the insurance company, you would be selling 45-day insurance contracts. That's the most optimal timeframe for the premium to have decayed without having any car accidents by the options buyer, which would have cost you, the option seller.

Theta

So that's an easy way to think about Theta. It's essentially like an insurance contract.

The further out in time you go, the more expensive Theta is. It is because there are more potential problems for the options seller just due to the very nature of holding the contract for a longer amount of time.

Theta will decline to zero from the moment you put it on until expiration. This is exactly what an option seller wants to happen, but the opposite of what an options buyer wants to happen.

Vega

Vega is something that can change very quickly with an options price, and it is definitely something you need to be aware of either buying or selling options.

It is the implied volatility price of an option. It's how much the options price will change (either up or down) with a one-point change in implied volatility.

Vega is the implied volatility value of an option.

Now, let's back up two seconds here and talk about implied volatility. Implied volatility is a potential movement range of a stock price. That could be up or down, or it could sit still.

Implied volatility can expand and it can contract, sometimes very quickly within a matter of minutes.

For an option seller, you want to sell it when implied volatility is high (when the Vega is high) and have a smaller-than-expected move. For an option buyer, you want to buy it when the Vega is low (when the implied volatility is low) and then have a bigger move than expected.

Now I've seen this firsthand, and I've traded both sides of this. When implied volatility suddenly spikes up, your stock price may not have moved all that much; but all of a sudden, there's an anticipated move that's baked in (maybe an earnings event or maybe some news leaked, causing investors to panic buy or sell).

Implied volatility generally increases as the price of the underlying stock decreases. While that may not always be the case, usually as prices go down volatility goes up because the movements are so much bigger. There's an old saying that stock prices take the stairs up and the elevator down.

Looking at Figure 9, a chart of SPY at the end of 2017, we see very small *baby* candles going up (they're so cute when they're so small), this is a representation of low implied volatility. In fact, the VIX, the CBOE Volatility Index measures the expected price changes in the S&P 500 Index options over the next 30 days, which hit historical lows during this period.

Figure 9:

Then all of a sudden in February 2018, everything just fell apart, and you'll see these humongous candles as shown in Figure 10. **It's not only "down" candles. It's also "up" candles.** These aren't so cute anymore!

Figure 10

Some of the biggest rallies ever happened in a bear market.

That's because prices are moving so much faster than they ever were in a bull market, and a lot of that has to do with fewer participants in a bear market and a bull market. Because if there are fewer people, prices have to move further in order for a buyer or a seller to be found. **This is what causes higher volatility, leading to higher implied volatility leading to higher options prices due to higher Vega.**

So what is a classic example of what you would want to happen as an option buyer? Let's say you buy an out of the money put for $1, and then the price of the stock goes down.

Well, that's good for your put. If the price of the stock goes down the implied volatility would generally go up. So, you have a double whammy that's working in your favor.

The price is moving in your direction, and volatility is also moving in your direction. You've bought that put option and you want the price of the put option to go up as the underlying price goes down. This is going to help that a lot.

Now let's say you're an option seller, and you've *sold* that put. It may still be out of the money, but (because the implied volatility has gone up because the price of the underlying has come down) that's going to be hard on that put you've sold as the price has risen.

Now with Vega, what you've got to be aware of is that this is trying to capture the *potential movement risk* based inside the options price. We've already covered Delta, and Delta is the actual underlying price movement baked into the options price.

We've covered theta which is the time value.

Now Vega is the potential movement risk that's built in the options price. As the seller, you want that to be high, but you also want to be far away from the money if it is high. As a buyer, you want to be close to the money and have a low Vega.

Vega

Just remember, with Vega if you're selling options you want to be high. If you're buying options, you want it to be low. It's as simple as that. **Vega is pricing into the option the expected potential range of that stock price over the life of the option contract period.**

Beta-Weighted Delta

We're going to be talking about Beta-Weighted Deltas. Now, we're going to be combining a few things here. Personally, I feel that Beta-Weighted Delta is one of the more important aspects that you should consider in your trading.

Beta-Weighted Delta combines the underlying change with its relative volatility to the market.

So previously, we've talked about Delta. That's the change in the options price for every one dollar move in the underlying stock price.

Okay, so that's Delta. So that's part of the equation. Then, we need to talk about the Beta. There's a Beta for every stock out there, and you can find that on any trading platform. You can even find it out on Yahoo Finance, CNBC, etc.

You just go to the underlying stock's information section, and it shows you all kinds of useful information including Beta.

Let's say, for example, you wanted to trade Amazon, and you wanted to know what Amazon's Beta was. Well, the Beta is important because it's going to give you an idea of how much it's going to move. (An idea of what its expected volatility range may be.)

So Beta, let's call it a 1.50 for Amazon. That means it's 50% more volatile than the overall market. So let's say, for example, if the market were to move one dollar, Amazon may move $1.50. If that Beta were 1.10 maybe the market would move a dollar, and your underlying would move to $1.10.

It can go the other way too. Let's say we're talking about something that's relatively small, relatively not in the news right now, and not a big growth stock like Amazon. Say we're talking about something like Ford. Maybe, its Beta is at .89. So while the market may move one dollar, Ford may move $0.89. So it gives you relative volatility to go along with the market.

Right, so now we're going to combine both the Delta from earlier and the Beta. So our Beta-Weighted Delta. Putting those two together gives you an overall look at your portfolio.

Now, of course, the markets will move, and that's something you need to keep in mind in your portfolio. Then, if you have a positive Beta-Weighted Delta, you're going to want the market to move up. If you have a negative Beta-Weighted Delta, you're going to want the market to move down.

With the Beta-Weighted Delta, you're going to have a result measured in Deltas. So let's say your Beta-Weighted Delta is Beta-Weighted to the S&P 500.

If you have a positive S&P 500, Beta-Weighted Delta it would be something like positive 5. Let's say if the S&P 500 went up one, your Beta-Weighted Delta showing a positive 5 would actually show your account would grow by $5.

Let's say the S&P 500 went down by 1. Then (your Beta-Weighted Delta being positive 5) your portfolio would actually go down by $5. **So it gives you an idea of what kind of market risk you have.**

By combining the Delta (the underlying change) with the Beta (the underlying relative volatility to the market), that gives you the Beta-Weighted Delta. This is something really crucial to keep in mind.

You can assign whatever you think is the most appropriate Beta-Weighted Delta for you. In a bull market, it may make sense to carry positive Deltas. In a bear market, it may make sense to carry negative Deltas. Whatever works for your risk tolerance and in your experience is really what you should be putting on for these.

Beta-Weighted Delta

So that wraps up the Beta-Weighted Delta. It's combining the market moves along with your own portfolio moves together to get an idea of how your portfolio would react based on changes in the market. It's really crucial to keep this in mind and keep it in the right proximity of the portfolio that you want to keep.

Do you want a bullish portfolio? Do you want a bearish portfolio? Do you want a neutral portfolio? Whatever works for you.

Gamma

We are going to cover the remaining Greeks that matter, these are less significant to a trader's portfolio, but useful to know.

Gamma is essentially the acceleration risk associated with Delta. The textbook definition of Gamma is:

Gamma is the rate that Delta will change based on a one dollar change in the stock price.

So, if Delta is the speed at which the option changes, you can think of Gamma as the acceleration. Gamma is the second derivative of Delta.

Gamma measures how much each Delta will change for every one dollar change in the stock.

So hear me out, I'm going to say it one more time. *Gamma* is the amount each *Delta* will move for every one dollar change in the stock.

If your car is moving at 50 miles an hour, let's say that's your Delta. For every one dollar move in the underlying stock, the price of the option will change by 50 cents, and you start applying the accelerator. So now your Gamma is actually changing the Delta from 50 to 52 from 52 to 53 from 53 to 55. The change from 50 to 50 to 52 to 53 and 53 to 55 is your Gamma. So, your Gamma is the small incremental changes between each delta point.

Now Gamma is great if you're selling options and you're right. But, Gamma is really bad if you're selling options and you're wrong, especially as you get closer to expiration.

Gamma will start to grow very quickly as expiration draws near, and that's what option sellers refer to as **Gamma risk.** As the option contract gets closer to expiration, Gamma starts to get bigger on those near the money options.

If I have something that's one strike out of the money and it may expire later today, there's a high Gamma risk there because at any point in time that Delta could go in the money.

Then, all of a sudden, my profitable trade has become unprofitable almost immediately as soon as that changes and goes into the money. So, Gamma risk starts to expand as you get closer to expiration. So as an option seller, that's why we want to be sure we can close those early.

Depending on the trade, I usually look to close or roll out to a longer-dated expiration several days before expiration. That gives me enough time to where I'm not worried about if it is or isn't going to be in the money at expiration. Hopefully, I've already taken my profits and moved on to the next trade.

Alpha

So next, we're going to be talking about Alpha. Essentially, it's how much better your asset (your portfolio, your fund, your stock, or whatever the case may be) outperforms its benchmark.

Alpha is the rate of return in excess of the market benchmark.

Let's say I was managing a hedge fund, and I consistently delivered positive Alpha.

That means I have consistently outperformed my benchmark.

Now my benchmark is subjective. I could choose the S&P 500. I could choose the Nasdaq. I could choose anything. I could choose Amazon if I wanted to, but a 1.0 Alpha means I've outperformed the benchmark index by 1%.

A negative 1.0 Alpha means I have underperformed the benchmark by 1%. **Alpha just gives you an idea of how well your asset is doing relative to your market index.**

Beta

Now, we talked about Beta before with Beta-Weighted Delta. Betas are essentially how volatile your stock is compared to the benchmark index.

Beta measures the stock's volatility in relation to the market.

Alpha is your returns overall, but Beta tells you your volatility. So **if you had a stock that had a Beta of 1.5, that means the stock is going to move 50% more than the benchmark does.**

If the S&P 500 goes up 1, your XYZ stock may go up 1.50, and if the S&P 500 goes down 1, it may go down 1.50. Now, that's similar to Alpha, but we're talking about intraday, intra-month, and intra-year volatility.

Whereas, we're not talking about from start to finish how well that performed relative to each other. **We're talking about the volatility day to day and how things are moving in correlation with each other.**

Rho

The last option Greek you're probably going to ever hear when you talk about them is Rho.

Rho is the amount the option value will change based on a one percentage point change in market interest rates.

We've actually seen several periods of rising rate environments for the overall market, but option contracts (unless you're dealing with massive scale) are not going to be impacted by this.

If they are, it's incredibly marginal. Because the changes are so small, Rho is an option's Greek that really does not get a lot of attention because of a couple of factors.

The market interest rate changes don't change all that frequently, and when they do, they're baked across every options' price. So, it's not an individual thing.

Number two is that it's such a small component of your options price overall; that it really has a negligible impact on your overall price. I mean it's marginal. It's tiny. But, it's so tiny, it's highly unlikely (but theoretically possible) to make or break any options trade you may put on.

Conclusion

I was once having a conversation with a very smart individual who tried to quiz me and ask me to recount the Black Scholes option pricing model math to him.

I said, "Why? None of that really matters, here's what you should care about..." and I listed off everything that's in this guide.

I have no desire to learn or teach how much Gamma sprinkled in with a little bit of Theta minus two thirds of a cup of Vega gives you one half Delta.

There are two things I want to know when I'm talking about Greeks. How much risk can I take and am I being rewarded appropriately for doing so?

After I explained each Greek in detail, that person replied with, "Yeah, you're just trying to sound smart..." *What?* Didn't you just try to make me look dumb by not knowing the theoretical pricing model? Ok buddy...

Now listen, if you take all of the information in this guide and apply it to your portfolio, you will have a much better idea on what risk and rewards are showing on the screen without having to guess. Everything you could ever want to know is there.

You may have to reach out to your individual broker platform's support desk to enable these numbers on your screen, but they are in all the option chains available on every platform, so any broker should be able to display these numbers.

With this guide, you now have all the truly necessary Greeks to trade faster and trade smarter. I'm confident that you will develop your own set of skills to become a successful options trader too!

Chapter 5

The Definitive Guide to Bullish Options Strategies

Ways to Potentially Profit from an Increase in an Underlying Stock Price

Foreword

"The Definitive Guide to Bullish Options Strategies" is designed to help you leverage the strategic advantages of options trading for making HIGH PROBABILITY bullish trades.

I've dedicated over a decade of my life to learning the ins and outs of trading stocks and options. In this guide, I aim to share some of the most valuable lessons I've gained through my experiences. I've made my fair share of mistakes and paid a significant amount of "trader tuition." My hope is that this chapter will contribute to your trading journey by allowing you to benefit from my successes and avoid repeating the same errors.

Thank you so much for taking the time to read this chapter!

Christopher M. Uhl, CMA

Introduction

Bullish trades are most suitable when the price of the underlying stock is expected to rise.

While there's an unlimited number of ways to combine calls and puts to create new strategies, these are the easiest and most useful for nearly every portfolio.

Each trade type presented in this guide has an ideal scenario. Knowing the trade setups is only part of the equation for making successful trades. Knowing when to enter, when to exit, and under what market scenario to do both is critical.

There is no silver bullet in trading. Although options offer the flexibility to be wrong to a certain degree, nothing is more important than risk management. As Warren Buffett would say, "Rule number one in making money is not to lose money. Rule number two is to refer to rule number one."

The Short Put Spread
BULLISH STRATEGY
aka Bull Put Spread, Put Credit Spread

Max Profit:	Credit Received
Max Risk:	Width of Strikes - Credit Received
Ideal Setup:	High IVR, Sell OTM Put & Buy Further OTM Put

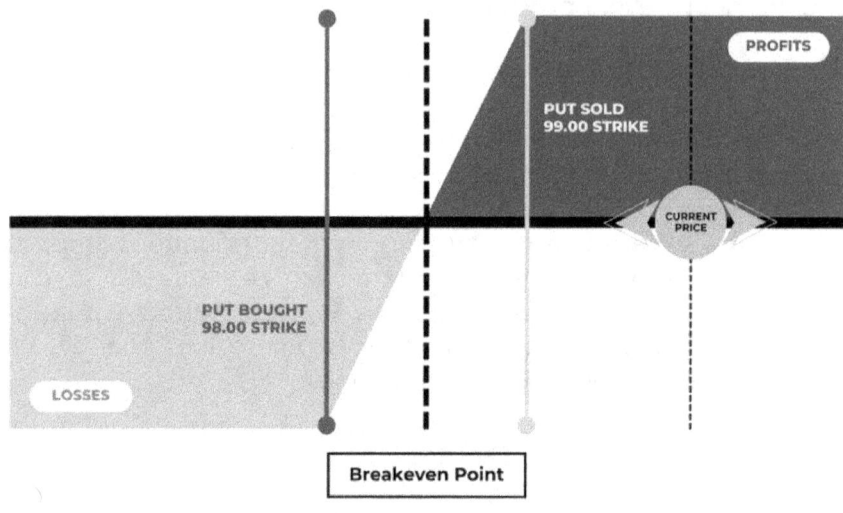

Breakeven Point

Put Sold Strike - Credit Received
99.00 - 0.25 = 98.75

Figure 1

The short put spread, one of the most basic high probability options trading strategies, is one I use all the time.

When you hear the word "short" that means you're selling something, in this case, you're selling a put and buying another put. Don't be too concerned with the buying and selling aspect of the trade setup. When you're selling the put spread, it's a bullish position, if you're buying the put spread, it's a bearish position. The buy or sell aspect of this trade is just your market assumption, it's not necessarily that you are stealing something and then selling it, it is merely just the stance you're taking and you are taking credit for doing so.

With this strategy, you would be selling an out of the money put, in Figure 1 it's the 99 put then buying a further out of the money put, the 98 put in this example shown above. The put that you've sold is worth more than the put that you've bought so you end up with a credit on the trade.

Ideal Setup

- Max Profit: Credit Received
- Max Risk: Width of Strikes – Credit Received
- High IV Rank
- Sell OTM Put & Buy Further OTM Put

Profit Targets

- 50% of credit received or
- Close or roll by 21 Days until expiration
- Reduces risk and increases win rates

Breakeven Points

- Put Sold Strike – Credit Received (Example: 99.00 – 0.25 = 98.75)

The Long Call Spread

BULLISH STRATEGY

aka Bull Call Spread, Put Debit Spread

Max Profit: Width of Strikes - Debit Paid
Max Risk: Debit Paid
Ideal Setup: Low IVR, Sell ATM Call & Buy ITM Call

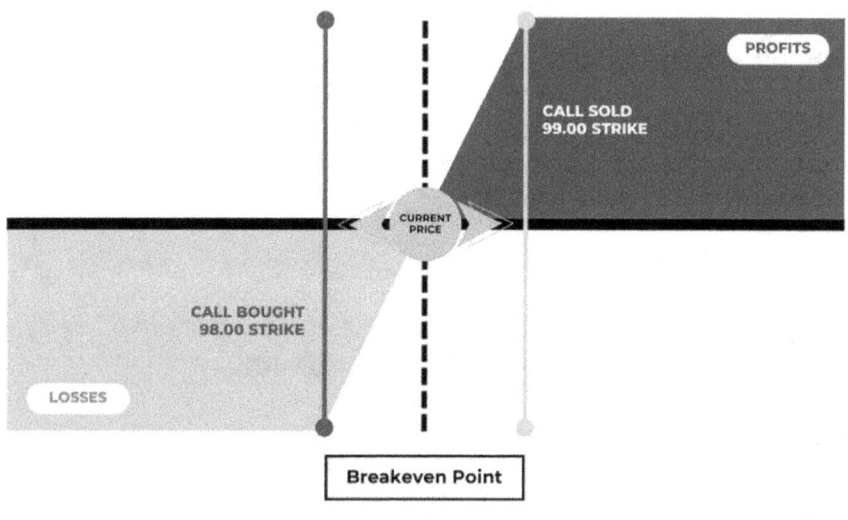

Breakeven Point

Call Bought Strike + Debit Paid
98.00 + 0.50 = 98.50

Figure 2

The long call spread, one of the most basic high probability options trading strategies, is one I use all the time.

When you hear the word "long" that means you're buying something, in this case, you're buying a call and selling another call. Don't be too concerned with the buying and selling aspect of the trade setup. When you're buying the call spread, it's a bullish position, if you're selling the call spread, it's a bearish position. The buy or sell aspect of this trade is just your market assumption, it's not necessarily that you are buying something from someone's inventory, it is merely just the stance you're taking and you are paying a debit to enter the trade.

With this strategy, you would be buying an in the money call, in Figure 2 below, it's the 98 call then selling an at the money call, the 99 call in this example shown above. The call you've bought is worth more than the call that you've sold so you end up with a debit on the trade.

Ideal Setup

- Max Profit: Width of Strikes – Debit Paid
- Max Risk: Debit Paid
- Low IV Rank
- Buy ITM Call & Sell ATM Call

Profit Targets

- 50% of debit paid or
- Close or roll by 21 Days until expiration (roll might be for a very small debit of 5 cents or less on this trade because it is a debit spread)
- Reduces risk and increases win rates

Breakeven Points

- Call Bought Strike + Debit Paid (Example: 98.00 + 0.50 = 98.50)

The Broken Wing Put Butterfly
BULLISH STRATEGY

Broken Wing Put Butterfly

Max Profit:	Width of Narrower Spread + Credit Received
Max Risk:	Sold Strike - Wider Spread Strike + Credit Received
Ideal Setup:	High IVR, Buy 1 OTM Put, Sell 2 Farther OTM Puts, Buy 1 Farther OTM Put

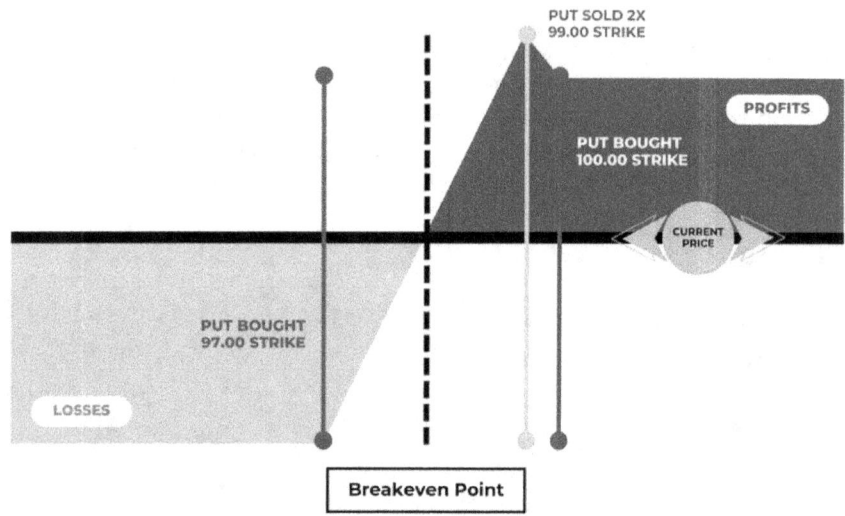

Put Sold Strike - Width of Narrower Spread - Credit Received
99.00 - 1.00 - 0.50 = 97.50

Figure 3

Broken wing butterflies are one of the most versatile trades that I like to deploy in my portfolio. It can be managed for a percentage of the credit received, held to expiration to try to hit the sweet spot where the profit is the highest, or it's possible to even roll up the longer side to make a risk free trade! (which is my personal favorite way to manage this)

The setup here is key, you must take in a credit in order to structure this trade in a way that has a profitable side. If this trade is structured for a debit, the probability of profit drops dramatically.

The broken wing butterfly takes the principle of selling two strikes and buying two more but adjusts the side farthest from the money, changing the risk profile and adding a higher probability of success. With this strategy, you would be selling 2 out of the money puts, buying 1 put 1 strike away, closer to the money then buying 1 put 2 strikes away, further from the money. The width can be varied, but the point is to have the side farther from the money be a wider spread than the side closer to the money all for a credit.

Ideal Setup

- Max Profit: Width of Narrower Spread + Credit Received
- Max Risk: Sold Strike – Wider Spread Strike + Credit Received
- High IV Rank
- Sell 2 OTM Puts, Buy 1 Closer to the Money Put 1 Strike Away from the Sold Puts, Buy 1 Further Out of the Money Put at Least
- 2 Strikes Away from the Sold Puts

Profit Targets

- 50% of Credit Received -or-
- Close or Roll by 21 Days until Expiration
- Reduces Risk and Increases Win Rates

Breakeven Points

- Put Sold Strike – Width of Narrower Spread – Credit Received
- Example: 99.00 – 1.00 – 0.50 = 97.50

The Better Call
BULLISH STRATEGY
Better Call

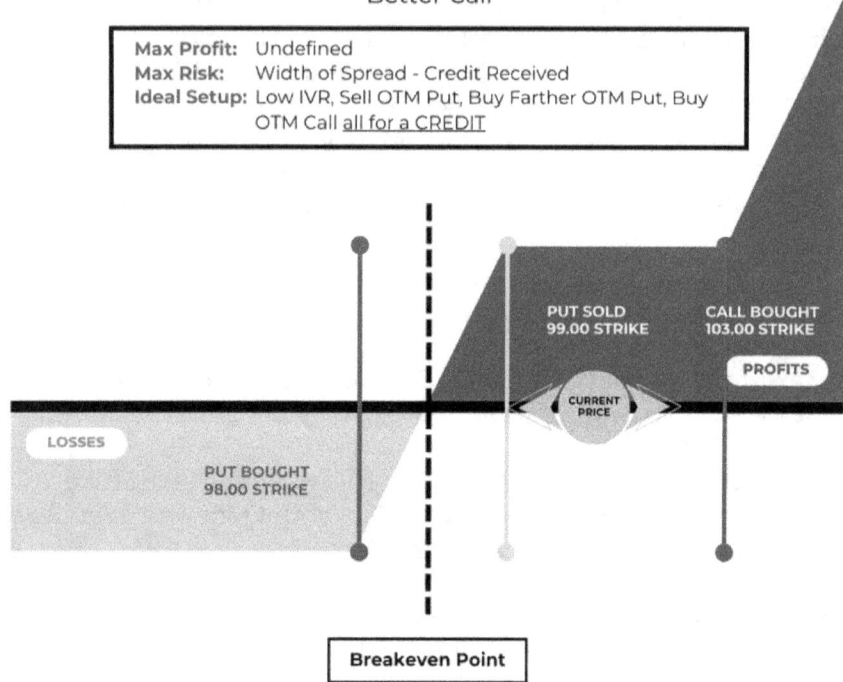

Max Profit: Undefined
Max Risk: Width of Spread - Credit Received
Ideal Setup: Low IVR, Sell OTM Put, Buy Farther OTM Put, Buy OTM Call <u>all for a CREDIT</u>

PUT SOLD
99.00 STRIKE

CALL BOUGHT
103.00 STRIKE

PROFITS

CURRENT PRICE

LOSSES

PUT BOUGHT
98.00 STRIKE

Breakeven Point

Put Sold Strike - Credit Received
99.00 - 0.15 = 98.85

Figure 4

I'm telling you, if I had figured out this Better Call strategy when I first started trading, I would have not lost so much money learning from experience.

This trade combines the best aspects of options trading: limited risk, high probability, and unlimited upside potential. In my opinion, this is the most advantageous options combination I have found. It can be managed to eliminate all risk in the trade, leaving only the long call, making a compelling case for being a significant game-changer in your portfolio.

A long call has theoretically unlimited profit potential, but it's only profitable after the strike goes in the money and surpasses the breakeven point. With the Better Call strategy, we are moving the breakeven point lower than the current price of the stock, allowing the trade to be profitable even if the stock remains still, goes up, or goes down to the breakeven.

This strategy addresses a common challenge with long calls – they expire worthless if they are out of the money. However, with this trade, if it's out of the money and above the breakeven point, it will expire, and you can still keep the entire credit taken in on the trade.

Here's how the strategy works: you sell an out-of-the-money put spread and then use the credit received to buy a long call. The final price of the trade should be a credit above the cost of your broker's commissions, ensuring profitability if all the strikes expire out of the money.

Ideal Setup:
- Max Profit: Undefined
- Max Risk: Width of Spread – Credit Received
- Low IV Rank
- Sell OTM Put, Buy Further OTM Put, Buy OTM Call All for a Credit

Profit Targets:
- Subjective, as the long call has undefined profit potential
- Laddered adjustment approach: Close or roll by 21 days until expiration to reduce risk and increase win rates.

Breakeven Points:
- Put Sold Strike – Credit Received
- Example: 99.00 – 0.15 = 98.85

The Long Call

BULLISH STRATEGY

Long Call

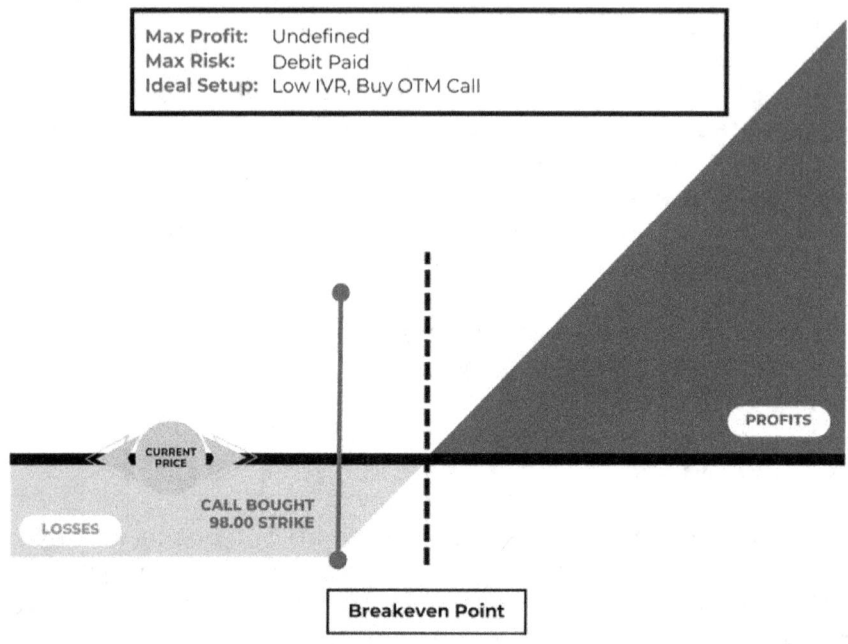

Max Profit:	Undefined
Max Risk:	Debit Paid
Ideal Setup:	Low IVR, Buy OTM Call

PROFITS

CURRENT PRICE

CALL BOUGHT
98.00 STRIKE

LOSSES

Breakeven Point

Call Bought Strike + Debit Paid
98.00 + 1.50 = 99.50

Figure 5

The long call is the most basic and original options trade. Imagine it being your lottery ticket, you buy a ticket for $1 and the next thing you know, you've hit the jackpot and the stock soars to infinity. Obviously that'll never happen, but that's the idea behind the long call.

By buying the call, you're placing a bet that the stock will go up and above the strike that you've purchased. You control 100 shares for only pennies on the dollar of buying the stock outright.

Here's the problem, if the stock never goes above your strike price, the option you bought is worthless, as in worth $0.00. Compare this with stock and you can see that when you liquidate your stock holding, you still have the equity value of the shares, the long call can be worth nothing if it's out of the money.

This is the reason people associate options trading with risky trading. And it's one of the reasons I learned some very expensive lessons when I first started trading and why I developed the better call.

This is in its nature a low probability trade and one I don't use except if I've made an adjustment, leaving a long call as a leftover trade.

Ideal Setup

- Max Profit: Undefined
- Max Risk: Debit Paid
- Low IV Rank
- Buy OTM Call

Profit Targets

- Subjective as the profit potential is undefined
- Close or roll by 21 days until expiration
- Reduces risk and increases win rates

Breakeven Points

- Call Bought Strike + Debit Paid
- Example: 98.00 + 1.50 = 99.50

Conclusion

No trader ever was 100% profitable all the time. There will be times when putting on a bullish trade seemed like the best idea, only for the market to reverse moments later.

Keeping the size of the trades small and the risk of financial ruin low is paramount when trading. Risk management should be the number one priority for the trader, well above and beyond capital growth.

When I trade options, I generally risk 3-5% of my account size in any one trade on the initial margin. So, if I have a $1,000 account, that means I will place a trade that takes the initial margin of $60-$80.

But I make sure that I only actually risk about half that much before I close the trade, before being "stopped out." There's no sense in holding a trade until expiration as a full loser if you can close early and eliminate half of the risk.

So, my initial margin percentage of 3-5% and 1.5-2.5% have a realized max loss of only 1.5%-2.5%. That means I would have to get 25 to 33 trades in a row back to back to blow up my account, which is highly unlikely, especially when trading high-probability setups as described in this guide.

With this guide, you now have the framework to know how to set up and manage bullish options strategies. With practice, experience, and a few expensive lessons, I'm confident you will develop your own set of skills to become a successful options trader too!

Chapter 6

**The Definitive Guide to Neutral
Options Strategies**

Ways to Potentially Profit from a Sideways Move in an Underlying Stock Price

Foreword

"Wait a minute, you're telling me I can have a winning trade if a stock doesn't move?

How is that even possible?"

This is the exact thought that ran through my head when I first heard about an Iron Condor. I honestly couldn't sleep that night, thinking about how this is going to impact my trading.

Neutral strategies are great, and many options traders will sing their praises, but I would like to give my personal experience with these.

I traded Iron Condors for years. They were my go-to trade, the one I always put on any chance I had, until I did an analysis on my portfolio...

While Iron Condors (I thought were paying me handsomely) had a win rate of over 80%, they had to be paying me, right? In fact, no, the losers were less frequent than the winners, but each of the losers was at a much larger dollar amount than the winners. In fact, 90% of my loss dollars came from Iron Condors, even when they had an 80% win rate. How is that even possible?

The credit taken in on an Iron Condor, or any trade for that matter, can be much lower than the amount of risk. For example, on a $5.00 wide Iron Condor, I may take $1.00 in credit, yet I've got $4.00 of risk. And if you don't manage that risk well, it can very quickly turn into a highly unprofitable trade.

Stocks move. This is a fact. Neutral strategies are aiming to take advantage of a stock not moving. Managing the risk so that you have a high win rate combined with small losses is key to making these trades successful.

Christopher M. Uhl, CMA

Introduction

Neutral trades are best suited when the price of the underlying stock goes sideways.

Of course, there's an unlimited way of combining calls and puts to create new strategies, but we believe these are the easiest and most useful in our portfolio.

Each one of the trade types presented in this guide has an ideal scenario. Knowing the trade setups is only part of the equation for making successful trades. Knowing when to enter, when to exit, and under what market scenario to do both is critical.

There is no silver bullet when trading. Even though options provide the flexibility to be wrong to a degree, nothing is more important than risk management. As Warren Buffett would say, "Rule number one in making money is not to lose money. Rule number two is to refer to rule number one."

The Iron Condor
NEUTRAL STRATEGY
Iron Condor

Max Profit: Credit Received
Max Risk: Width of Strikes - Credit Received
Ideal Setup: High IVR, Sell OTM Call Spread & OTM Put Spread

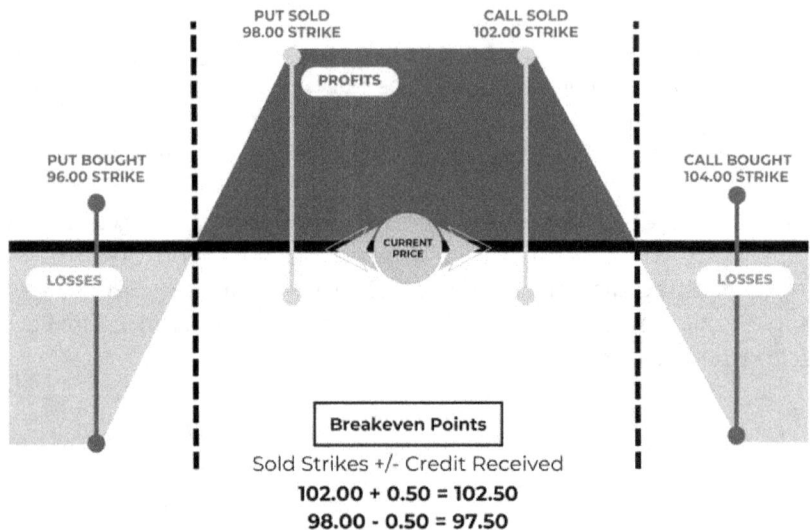

Figure 1

The Iron Condor trade is probably the most well-known neutral options trade and one I've had in my portfolio for years.

Why is it called an Iron Condor?

When a trade combines both a call spread and put spread, it's labeled "Iron." This trade, because of its wide wings (just like a condor), is thus labeled an Iron Condor since we are selling both a call and put spread. This is similar to the Iron Butterfly but generally has a higher probability of profit as the sold spreads are out of the money.

With the Iron Condor, we are effectively boxing in a trade. We are saying we feel that the price will be between these two points. Think of it like making a wager on the price of gas. I might wager that for the next 30 days, the price of gas will stay above $2.00 but less than $4.00, and if it goes beyond either of those two points, I'll lose the wager.

But that is where this is a powerful trade. You see with this trade, the stock price actually HAS TO DO SOMETHING. It has to move outside the range you've determined before expiration. And by using the delta values in the trade, we can determine the likelihood of that happening. Based on the options prices, you can determine your probability of profit before ever entering the trade.

To set up this trade, you would need to sell an out-of-the-money call spread and an out-of-the-money put spread. The farther out of the money you sell these two spreads, the higher the probability of profit you're likely to have.

Ideal Setup:
- Max Profit: Credit Received
- Max Risk: Width of Strikes – Credit Received
- High IV Rank
- Sell OTM Call Spread & Sell OTM Put Spread

Profit Targets:
- 50% of credit received or
- Close or roll by 21 Days until expiration
- Reduces risk and increases win rates

Break-even Points:
Two Break-even Points on this Trade:
- Sold Strikes +/- Credit Received
- Example: 102.00 + 0.50 = 102.50 and 98.00 – 0.50 = 97.50

The Iron Butterfly

NEUTRAL STRATEGY

Iron Butterfly

> **Max Profit:** Credit Received
> **Max Risk:** Width of Strikes - Credit Received
> **Ideal Setup:** High IVR, Sell ATM Call Spread & ATM Put Spread

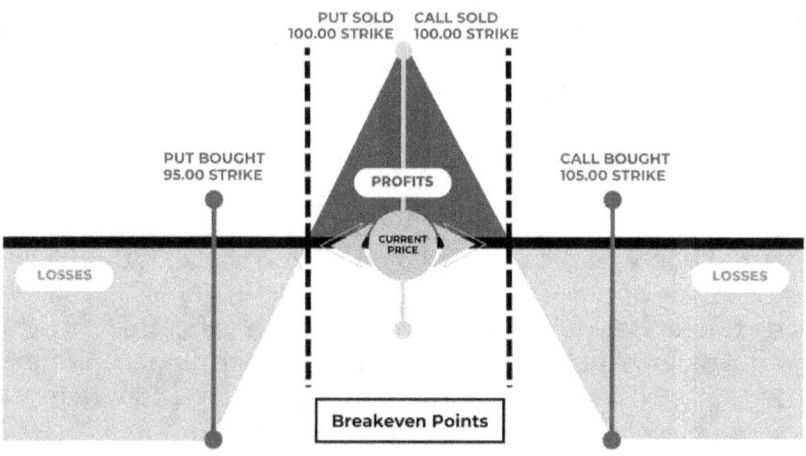

Sold Strikes +/- Credit Received
100.00 + 2.50 = 102.50
100.00 - 2.50 = 97.50

Figure 2

The Iron Butterfly trade is a very easy to use neutral options trade that takes advantage of the highest priced options, the at the money calls and puts.

Why is it called an Iron Butterfly?

When a trade combines both a call spread and put spread, it's labeled "Iron." This trade, because of its wings (just like a butterfly), is thus labeled an Iron Butterfly since we are selling both at-the-money call and put spreads. This is very similar to the Iron Condor, but that trade is set up with out-of-the-money spreads, whereas these are at the money.

With the Iron Butterfly, we are effectively boxing in a trade. We are saying we feel that the price will not move all that much before expiration. Think of it like making a wager on the price of gas. I might wager that for the next 30 days, the price of gas will stay around $3, and if it goes much farther than that, I'll lose the wager.

But that is where this is a powerful trade. You see, with this trade, the stock price actually HAS TO DO SOMETHING. It has to move outside the range you've determined before expiration. And because you've sold the highest-priced (extrinsic value) options in the chain, you're being compensated for taking on the risk. That compensation is what allows the break-even points to be somewhat distant from the strikes that were sold.

To set up this trade, you would need to sell an at-the-money call spread and an at-the-money put spread. The higher the price you can sell these two spreads for, the higher the probability of profit you're likely to have.

Ideal Setup:
- Max Profit: Credit Received
- Max Risk: Width of Strikes – Credit Received
- High IV Rank
- Sell ATM Call Spread & Sell ATM Put Spread

Profit Targets:
- 25% of the credit received or
- Close or roll by 21 Days until expiration
- Reduces risk and increases win rates

Break-even Points:
Two Break-even Points on this Trade:

- Sold Strikes +/- Credit Received
- Example: 100.00 + 2.50 = 102.50 and 100.00 – 2.50 = 97.50

The Long Straddle

NEUTRAL STRATEGY

Long Straddle

Max Profit:	Undefined
Max Risk:	Debit Paid
Ideal Setup:	Low IVR, Buy ATM Call & Put

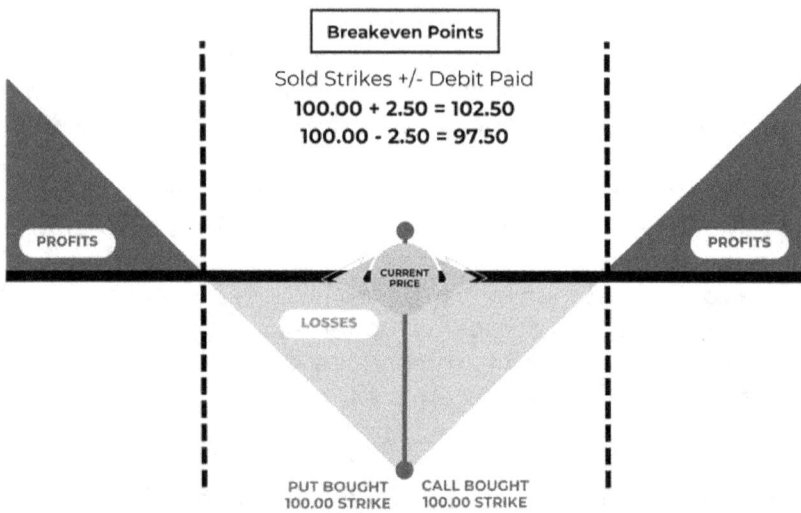

Breakeven Points

Sold Strikes +/- Debit Paid
100.00 + 2.50 = 102.50
100.00 - 2.50 = 97.50

PROFITS

PROFITS

CURRENT PRICE

LOSSES

PUT BOUGHT
100.00 STRIKE

CALL BOUGHT
100.00 STRIKE

Figure 3

The Long Straddle is one way to take advantage of large moves that you anticipate will happen in a stock in a short period of time. The only drawback to this strategy is that if the market also anticipates the large moves, then you'll have to pay more to enter the trade, therefore pushing your breakeven points further away from the current price.

Why is it named a Long Straddle?

This trade involves buying the at-the-money call and put, essentially straddling the current stock price across the options chain. Selling these two forms the short straddle.

With the long straddle, we bet on possessing superior insights into potential market movements compared to the overall market. We anticipate a significant impending move, possibly not yet factored into the options pricing. However, the direction of this move remains uncertain. This strategy gains popularity during earnings seasons when stocks often experience substantial volatility.

In contrast to the Iron Butterfly, the stock price must definitively move, and this movement must occur before expiration for the trade to yield profit. If the stock remains stagnant in the loss zone, the trade's value diminishes daily. Movement beyond the breakeven points' determined range before expiration is crucial.

To initiate this trade, purchase an at-the-money call and an at-the-money put. A lower cost for these two legs increases the likelihood of profitability.

Ideal Setup:
- Max Profit: Credit Received
- Max Risk: Width of Strikes – Credit Received
- Low IV Rank
- Buy ATM Call & Put

Profit Targets:

Subjective as the profit potential is undefined, close or roll by 21 days until expiration to reduce risk and increase win rates.

Breakeven Points:

Two Breakeven Points on this Trade
Bought Strikes +/- Credit Received
Example: 100.00 + 2.50 = 102.50 and 100.00 – 2.50 = 97.50

The Calendar Spread
NEUTRAL STRATEGY

Calendar Spread

Max Profit:	Somewhat Undefined
Max Risk:	Debit Paid
Ideal Setup:	Low IVR, Sell Call/Put in Front Month and Buy Call/Put in Back Month on Same Strike

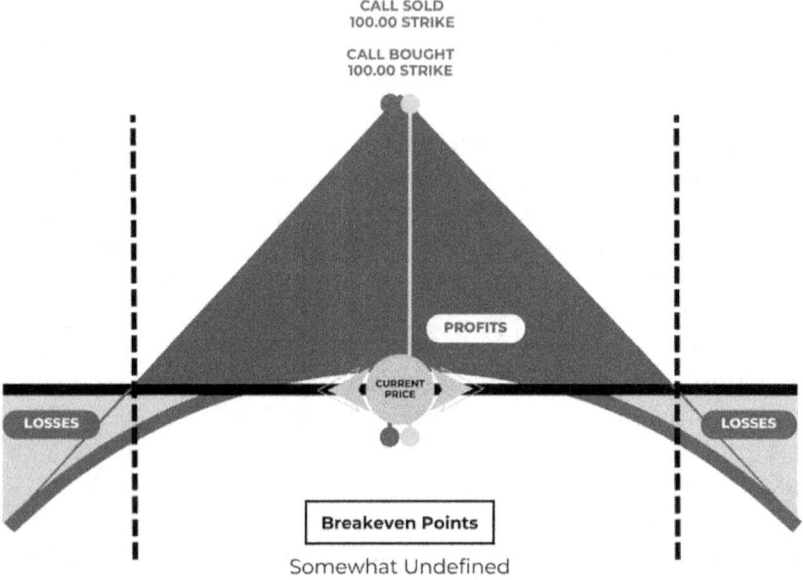

Figure 4

Calendar Spread: An Economical Neutral Trade for Options Pricing Increase

The calendar spread provides a cost-effective approach to execute a neutral trade, ideally positioned to capitalize on an upswing in options pricing.

Why is it called a Calendar Spread?

This strategy involves selling an at-the-money call or put and concurrently purchasing another call or put (ensuring they share the same strike) across two distinct time periods. Commonly, this entails selling the "front month" and buying the "back month," although the approach can be applied to any two time periods.

I typically stick to monthly contracts due to their superior liquidity, ensuring a minimum of one month between them. For instance, selling the October 100 Call and simultaneously buying the December 100 Call, with the intervening November call.

Crossing periods in this manner serves a defensive purpose. If the trade isn't profitable by October expiration, I can roll the October strike to November, gaining credit to offset the initial debit. Rolling within the same month and strike is not viable, as it would close the trade.

This strategy mirrors the risk profile of an Iron Butterfly.

Setup:
- Max Profit: Somewhat Undefined
- Max Risk: Debit Paid
- Low IV Rank
- Sell ATM Call/Put in Front Month & Buy ATM Call/Put in Back Month

Profit Targets:
- 10-20% of Debit Paid
- Close or roll by 21 Days until expiration of the front-month contract to reduce risk and enhance win rates

Breakeven Points:
Somewhat Undefined The break-even for a calendar spread cannot be accurately calculated due to the different expiration cycles used and changes in volatility between the two time period's contracts.

The Double Calendar

NEUTRAL STRATEGY

Double Calendar Spread

Max Profit:	Somewhat Undefined
Max Risk:	Debit Paid
Ideal Setup:	Low IVR, Sell Call/Put in Front Month and Buy Call/Put in Back Month on Same Strike 2x

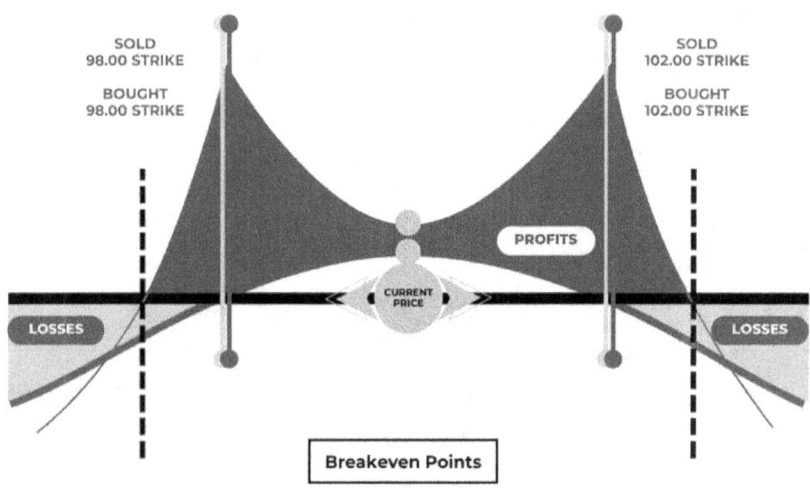

Figure 5

The double calendar spread combines two calendar spreads in a cost-effective manner, offering an ideal approach for a neutral trade that leverages potential increases in options pricing.

Why is it called a Double Calendar Spread?

This trade involves selling an at-the-money call or put and then buying another call or put (they need to stay the same) across two time periods, just like a regular calendar spread. However, we are now executing both a call and put spread instead of choosing between them. The goal is to set up a neutral trade across both sides of the money strikes and across time periods. Typically, this is referred to as selling the "front month" and buying the "back month," but it can be done across any two time periods.

I generally stick to monthly contracts as they are the most liquid, and I try to have at least one month in between. So, I could sell the October 100 Call and then buy the December 100 Call, leaving the November call in between.

The reason I cross periods like that is for defense. If the trade is not profitable by the time October expires, I can roll the strike from October to November and pick up some credit to offset the original debit I took in on the trade. I wouldn't be able to roll to the same month on the same strike, as that would close the trade.

This trade has a similar risk profile to that of an Iron Condor.

To set up this trade, you would need to sell an out-of-the-money call and put in a near-dated options chain and buy an out-of-the-money call and put in a further-dated options chain on the same strikes as the front month.

Ideal Setup:

- Max Profit: Somewhat Undefined
- Max Risk: Debit Paid
- Low IV Rank
- Sell OTM Call and Put in Front Month & Buy OTM Call and Put in
- Back Month

Profit Targets:

- 50% of Debit Paid
- Close or roll by 21 Days until expiration of front-month contract
- Reduces risk and increases win rates

Breakeven Points:

Somewhat Undefined

The break-even for a calendar spread cannot be accurately calculated due to the different expiration cycles being used and changes in volatility between the two time period's contracts.

Conclusion

No trader was ever 100% profitable all the time. There will be times where putting on a neutral trade seemed like the best idea, only for the market to take an unexpectedly large move moments later.

Keeping the size of the trades small and the risk of financial ruin minimal is paramount when trading. Risk management should be the number one priority to the trader, well above and beyond capital growth.

When I trade options, I generally trade 3-5% of my account size in any one trade on an initial margin. If I have a $1,000 account, that means I will place a trade that takes the initial margin of $60-$80.

But I make sure I only actually risk about half that much before I close the trade, before being "stopped out." There's no sense in holding a trade until expiration as a full loser if you can close early and eliminate half of the risk.

So my initial margin percentage of 3-5% and 1.5-2.5% has a realized max loss of only 1.5%-2.5%. That means I would have to get 25 to 33 trades in a row back to back to blow up my account, which is highly unlikely, especially when trading high-probability setups as described in this guide.

With this guide, you now have the framework to know how to set up and manage bearish options strategies. With practice, experience, and a few expensive lessons, I'm confident you will develop your own set of skills to become a OVTLYR Trader too!

Chapter 7

**The Definitive Guide to Bearish
Options Strategies**

Ways to Potentially Profit
from a Decrease in an
Underlying Stock Price

Foreword

I heard a stat one day that 80% of people do not know they can profit from a decline in the price of a stock. The question was asked, "How do you profit when a stock goes up?" The responses were to buy the stock, obviously. But when asked, "How do you profit when a stock goes down?" The responses were mixed, with most having a confused look on their face.

To be honest, I was in the second camp, and you may have been too up to a certain point in your life. I only recently had a conversation with a family member who had a similar epiphany, "You can make money when a stock goes down? How's that even possible?"

In this chapter, I'm going to show you five ways this is possible, all while having our risk defined. Stocks trade on a logarithmic scale; that's a fancy way of saying that they can only go to zero and no less. But they can go up to infinity.

This is where the danger lies for someone who wants to make a bearish trade. In this guide, every strategy has a max loss, so even if the stock you decided to short (meaning having a bearish bias towards) goes to infinity, you would have only limited losses.

Christopher M. Uhl, CMA

Introduction

Bearish trades are best suited when the price of the underlying stock goes down.

Of course, there's an unlimited way of combining calls and puts to create new strategies, but we believe these are the easiest and most useful in our portfolio.

We consistently use only about three strategies for bearish trades.

Those are the call credit spread, the put debit spread, and the call broken wing butterfly.

Each of the trade types presented in this guide has an ideal scenario. Knowing the trade setups is only part of the equation for making successful trades. Knowing when to enter, when to exit, and under what market scenario to do both is critical.

There is no silver bullet in trading, even though options provide the flexibility to be wrong to a degree. Nothing is more important than risk management. As Warren Buffett would say, "Rule number one in making money is not to lose money. Rule number two is to refer to rule number one."

The Short Call Spread
BEARISH STRATEGY
aka Bear Call Spread, Call Credit Spread

Max Profit:	Credit Received
Max Risk:	Width of Strikes - Credit Received
Ideal Setup:	High IVR, Sell OTM Call & Buy OTM Call

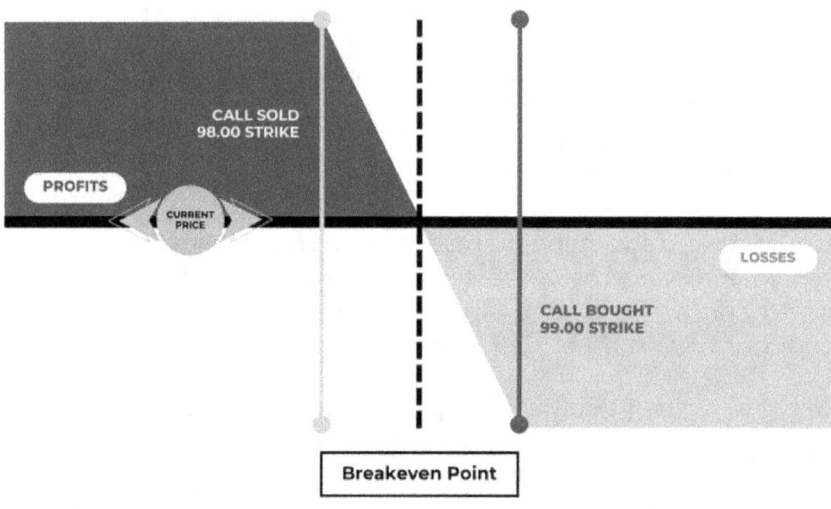

CALL SOLD
98.00 STRIKE

PROFITS

CURRENT PRICE

LOSSES

CALL BOUGHT
99.00 STRIKE

Breakeven Point

Call Sold Strike + Credit Received
98.00 + 0.25 = 98.25

The short call spread, one of the most basic high probability options trading strategies, is one I use all the time.

When you hear the word "short," that means you're selling something; in this case, you're selling a call and buying another call. Don't be too concerned with the buying and selling aspect of the trade setup. When you're selling the call spread, it's a bearish position; if you're buying the call spread, it's a bullish position.

The buy or sell aspect of this trade is just your market assumption; it's not necessarily that you are stealing something then selling it; it is merely just the stance you're taking, and you are taking credit for doing so.

With this strategy, you would be selling an out-of-the-money call. In the example above, it's the 98 call, then buying a further out-of-the-money call, the 99 call in this example shown above.

The call that you've sold is worth more than the call you've bought, so you end up with a credit on the trade.

Ideal Setup:
- Max Profit: Credit Received
- Max Risk: Width of Strikes – Credit Received
- High IV Rank
- Sell OTM Call & Buy Further OTM Call

Profit Targets:
- 50% of credit received or
- Close or roll by 21 Days until expiration
- Reduces risk and increases win rates

Breakeven Points:
Call Sold Strike + Credit Received Example: 98.00 + 0.25 = 98.25

The Long Put Spread
BEARISH STRATEGY
aka Bear Put Spread, Put Debit Spread

Max Profit: Width of Strikes - Debit Paid
Max Risk: Debit Paid
Ideal Setup: Low IVR, Sell ATM Put & Buy ITM Put

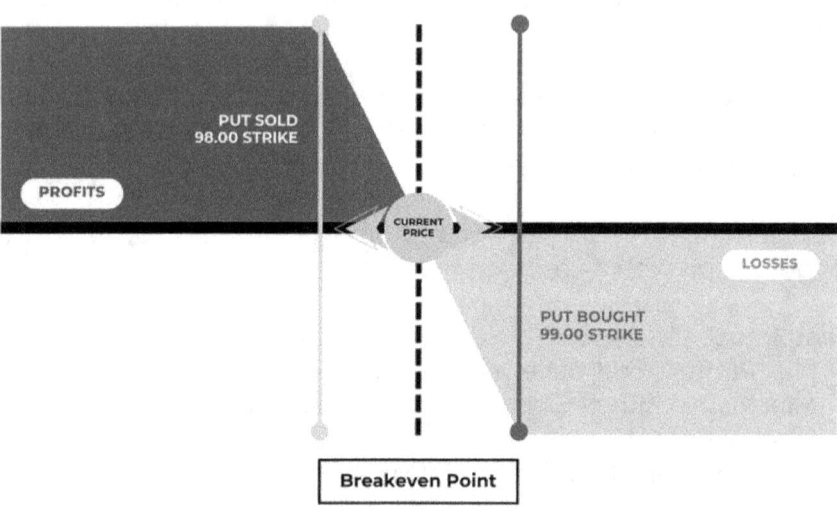

PROFITS

PUT SOLD
98.00 STRIKE

CURRENT
PRICE

LOSSES

PUT BOUGHT
99.00 STRIKE

Breakeven Point

Put Bought Strike - Debit Paid
99.00 - 0.50 = 98.50

The long put spread, one of the most basic high probability options trading strategies, is one I use all the time.

When you hear the word "long," that means you're buying something; in this case, you're buying a put and selling another put. Don't be too concerned with the buying and selling aspect of the trade setup. When you're buying the put spread, it's a bearish position; if you're selling the put spread, it's a bullish position. The buy or sell aspect of this trade is just your market assumption; it's not necessarily that you are buying something from someone's inventory; it is merely just the stance you're taking, and you are paying a debit to enter the trade.

With this strategy, you would be buying an in-the-money put; in the example above, it's the 99 put, then selling an at-the-money put, the 98 put in this example shown above. The put that you've bought is worth more than the put that you've sold, so you end up with a debit on the trade.

Ideal Setup:
- Max Profit: Width of Strikes – Debit Paid
- Max Risk: Debit Paid
- Low IV Rank
- Buy ITM Put & Sell ATM Put

Profit Targets:
- 50% of debit paid or
- Close or roll by 21 Days until expiration (roll might be for a very small debit of 5 cents or less on this trade because it is a debit spread)
- Reduces risk and increases win rates

Breakeven Points:
Put Bought Strike – Debit Paid Example: 99.00 – 0.50 = 98.50

The Broken Wing Call Butterfly

BEARISH STRATEGY

Broken Wing Call Butterfly

Max Profit:	Width of Narrower Spread + Credit Received
Max Risk:	Sold Strike - Wider Spread Strike + Credit Received
Ideal Setup:	High IVR, Buy 1 OTM Call, Sell 2 Farther OTM Calls, Buy 1 Farther OTM Call

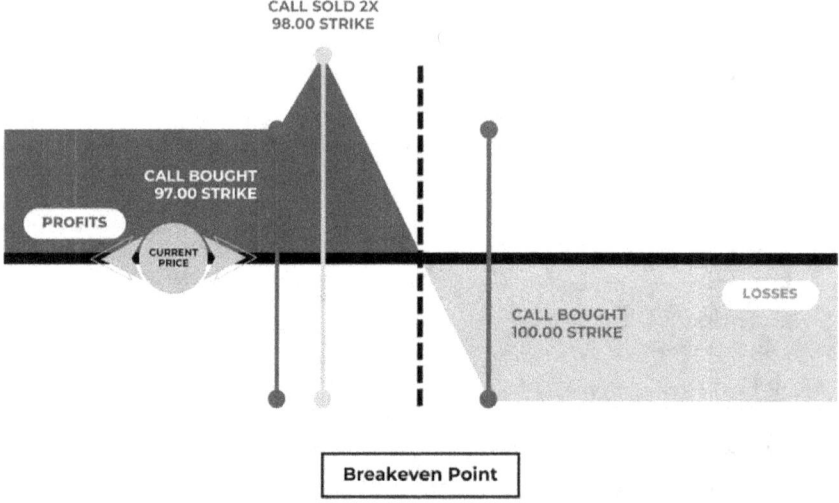

Breakeven Point

Call Sold Strike + Width of Narrower Spread + Credit Received
98.00 + 1.00 + 0.50 = 99.50

Broken wing butterflies are one of the most versatile trades that I like to deploy in my portfolio. It can be managed for a percentage of the credit received, held to expiration to try to hit the sweet spot where the profit is the highest, or it's possible to even roll up the longer side to make a risk-free trade! (which is my personal favorite way to manage this)

The setup here is key; you must take in a credit to structure this trade in a way that has a profitable side. If this trade is structured for a debit, the probability of profit drops dramatically. A regular butterfly trade, covered in the neutral strategies section, is structured where you sell 2 calls then buy one call on either side at equidistant strikes away from the sold strikes. It looks like a triangle without a bottom, as mentioned in the video above.

The broken wing butterfly takes the principle of selling two strikes and buying two more but adjusts the side farthest from the money, changing the risk profile and adding a higher probability of success.

With this strategy, you would be selling 2 out-of-the-money calls, buying 1 call 1 strike away, closer to the money, then buying 1 call 2 strikes away, further from the money. The width can be varied, but the point is to have the side farther from the money be a wider spread than the side closer to the money, all for a credit.

Ideal Setup:

- Max Profit: Width of Narrower Spread + Credit Received
- Max Risk: Sold Strike – Wider Spread Strike + Credit Received
- High IV Rank
- Sell 2 OTM Calls, Buy 1 Closer to the Money Call 1 Strike Away from the Sold Calls, Buy 1 Further Out of the Money Call at Least 2 Strikes Away from the Sold Calls

Profit Targets:

- 50% of Credit Received -or-
- Close or Roll by 21 Days until Expiration
- Reduces Risk and Increases Win Rates

Breakeven Points:

Call Sold Strike + Width of Narrower Spread + Credit Received
Example: 98.00 + 1.00 + 0.50 = 99.50

The Better Put

BEARISH STRATEGY

Better Put

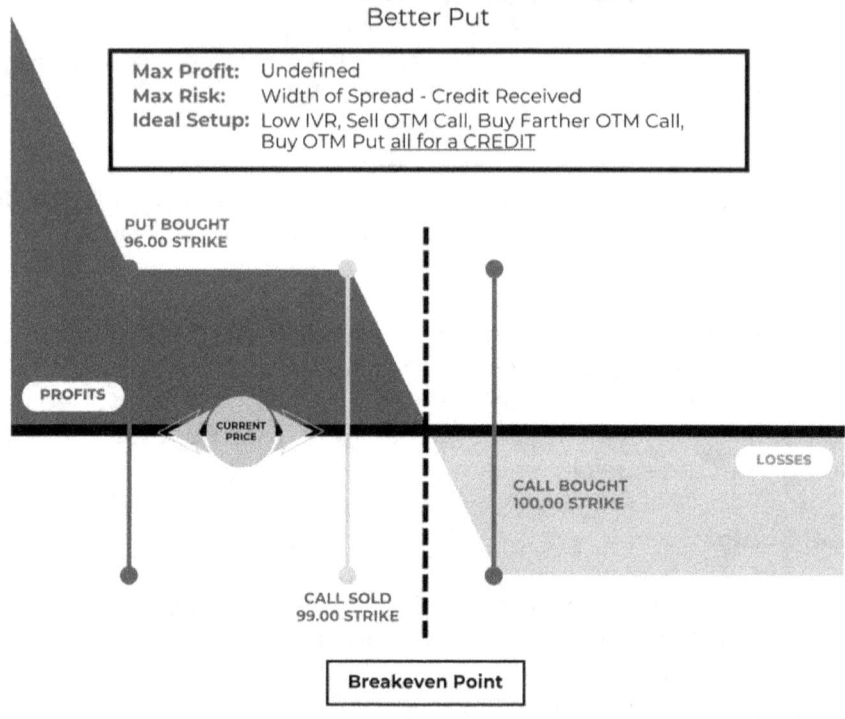

Max Profit:	Undefined	
Max Risk:	Width of Spread - Credit Received	
Ideal Setup:	Low IVR, Sell OTM Call, Buy Farther OTM Call, Buy OTM Put <u>all for a CREDIT</u>	

PUT BOUGHT
96.00 STRIKE

PROFITS

CURRENT
PRICE

LOSSES

CALL BOUGHT
100.00 STRIKE

CALL SOLD
99.00 STRIKE

Breakeven Point

Call Sold Strike + Credit Received
98.00 + 0.15 = 99.15

I'm telling you, if I had figured out this Better Put strategy when I first started trading, I would have not lost so much money learning from experience.

This trade combines the best of all the worlds of options trading: limited risk, high probability, and unlimited profit potential. In my opinion, this is the best combination of options I have been able to find.

And it can be managed to remove all risk in the trade and leave just the long put, for free, making an even stronger case about how this could be a huge game-changer for your portfolio.

A long put has theoretical unlimited profit potential as the price of the underlying stock could go all the way to zero, but it's only profitable after the strike goes in the money and surpasses the breakeven point. With the better put, we are moving the breakeven point above the current price of the stock, so the trade can sit still, go down, or even up to our breakeven, and it is still profitable.

This is where I could have used this strategy starting out. Long puts expire worthless if they are out of the money, but with this trade, if it's out of the money and below the breakeven point, it will expire, and you can still keep the entire credit taken in on the trade.

With this strategy, you would be selling an out-of-the-money call spread then buying a long put with the credit from the sale of the put spread. It's important that the final price of the trade be a credit above the cost of your broker's commissions so if all the strikes expire out of the money, the trade will be profitable.

Ideal Setup:

- Max Profit: Undefined
- Max Risk: Width of Spread – Credit Received
- Low IV Rank
- Sell OTM Call, Buy Further OTM Call, Buy OTM Put All for a Credit

Profit Targets:

- Subjective as the long put has undefined profit potential
- I have a laddered adjustment approach explained below
- Close or roll by 21 Days until expiration
- Reduces risk and increases win rates

Breakeven Points:

Call Sold Strike + Credit Received Example: 99.00 + 0.15 = 99.15

The Long Put

BEARISH STRATEGY

Long Put

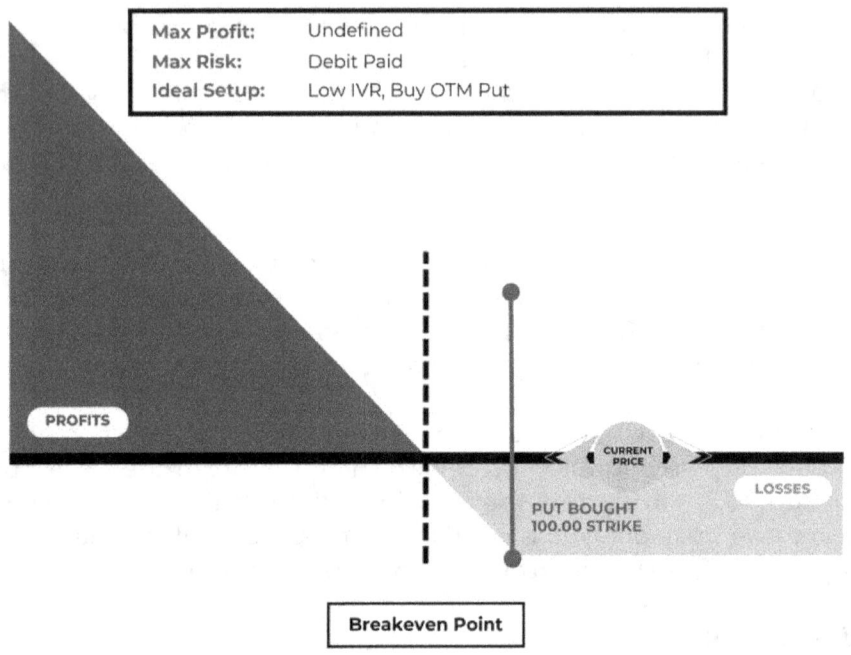

Max Profit:	Undefined
Max Risk:	Debit Paid
Ideal Setup:	Low IVR, Buy OTM Put

PROFITS

CURRENT PRICE

LOSSES

PUT BOUGHT
100.00 STRIKE

Breakeven Point

Put Bought Strike - Debit Paid
100.00 - 1.50 = 98.50

The long put is the most basic bearish options trade. Imagine it being your lottery ticket; you buy a ticket for $1, and the next thing you know, you've hit the jackpot, and the stock plummets to zero. This is theoretically more possible than the long call going to infinity as a company could go bankrupt or have devastating news, which is why these trade for a higher premium than long calls do.

By buying the put, you're placing a bet that the stock will go down and below the strike you've purchased. You control 100 shares for only pennies on the dollar of short selling the stock outright.

Here's the problem: if the stock never goes below your strike price, the option you bought is worthless, as in worth $0.00. Compare this with short or long stock, and you can see that when you liquidate your stock holding, you still have the equity value of the shares; the long put can be worth nothing if it's out of the money.

This is the reason people associate options trading with risky trading. And it's one of the reasons I learned some very expensive lessons when I first started trading and why I developed the better put.

This is, in its nature, a low-probability trade and one I don't use except if I've made an adjustment, leaving a long put as a leftover trade.

Ideal Setup:

- Max Profit: Undefined (to zero on the underlying stock)
- Max Risk: Debit Paid
- Low IV Rank
- Buy OTM Put

Profit Targets:

- Subjective as the profit potential is undefined
- Close or roll by 21 days until expiration
- Reduces risk and increases win rates

Breakeven Points:

Put Bought Strike – Debit Paid
Example: 100.00 – 1.50 = 98.50

Conclusion

No trader was ever 100% profitable all the time. There will be times where putting on a bearish trade seemed like the best idea, only for the market to reverse moments later.

Keeping the size of the trades small and the risk of financial ruin small is paramount when trading. Risk management should be the number one priority for the trader, well above and beyond capital growth.

When I trade options, I generally trade 3-5% and 1.5-2.5% of my account size in any one trade on the initial margin. So if I have a $1,000 account, that means I will place a trade that takes the initial margin of $60-$80.

But I make sure that I only actually risk about half that much before I close the trade, before being "stopped out." There's no sense in holding a trade until expiration as a full loser if you can close early and eliminate half of the risk.

So my initial margin percentage of 3.5% has a realized max loss of only 1.5%-2.5%. That means I would have to get 25 to 33 trades in a row back to back to blow up my account, which is highly unlikely, especially when trading high-probability setups as described in this guide.

With this guide, you now have the framework to know how to set up and manage bearish options strategies. With practice, experience, and a few expensive lessons, I'm confident that you will develop your own set of skills to become a OVTLYR Trader too!

Chapter 8

The Definitive Guide to Avoiding Pattern Day Trading Problems

3 Ways to Avoid Getting Your Account Locked Due to Pattern Day Trading Rules

Foreword

Getting hit with a pattern day trading rule just sucks. It happened to me, and I didn't see it coming because I had never heard of it.

When I got the call from Fidelity Investments, and they said my account had been locked for 90 days due to repeated violations of the pattern day trading rule, I was upset.

Why didn't anyone warn me?

What's going to happen to all these positions I have? Is this some kind of conspiracy?

You may have had similar thoughts the first time you were hit with this restriction. Thankfully, the conspiracy theory was short-lived, and I learned a few valuable lessons. I thought I could help newer traders so they know how to steer clear of this happening to their accounts.

Christopher M. Uhl, CMA

Introduction

In this guide, you'll find three ways to avoid pattern day trading restrictions. This is not meant to provide a guide to circumvent financial laws; it's a way to show you how to work within those laws and avoid running into trouble.

Everything in this guide has been learned from experience and is presented to help the reader learn without having to go through these experiences themselves.

3 Ways to Avoid Getting Your Account Locked Due to Pattern Day Trading Rules

If you have four or more day trades in any five-day period, meaning you enter and exit a single position in the same trading day, you are classified as a Pattern Day Trader.

While that on its own is not a bad thing, what happens because of the FINRA regulations on day trading can set you back up to 90 days.

Pattern Day Trading is defined by FINRA as: "any customer who executes four or more 'day trades' within five business days" (source: http://www.finra.org/investors/highlights/day-traders-mind-your-margin).

The rule specifically includes individuals with margin accounts with an equity value of less than $25,000.

The Pattern Day Trading Rule was created by FINRA in an effort to curb people trading themselves into bankruptcy.

The thought was that anyone with at least $25,000 could afford to get into and out of trades without too much risk of blowing up their account. Because, of course, they must be financially savvy enough to have saved $25,000 to use for trading in the first place (heavy sarcasm intended).

Brokers are required to lock your account for up to 90 days if a PDT violation has occurred.

Here are three ways to ensure you never run into the Pattern Day Trading rule:

1. Limit yourself to only two day trades in any given week (Monday to Friday).

Running into an issue with four or more trades in a given five-day period can be avoided by sticking to one day trade per day and a maximum of two in any calendar week.

For example, if you place one day trade on Monday and another on Thursday, you reach two day trades in a five-day period. You could even add a third day trade the following Monday, totaling three in a five-day window.

On the Tuesday of the subsequent week, the first day trade placed the previous Monday is no longer counted toward the three-in-five-days limit. However, you still have trades from last Thursday and this Monday within your PDT window.

The max two in a week rule should be the go-to for anyone with an account less than $25,000 looking to take advantage of intraday swings.

2. Hold trades overnight.

Holding your trade from one trading session to the next, from Monday to Tuesday or from Friday to Monday, ensures these trades are not counted as day trades. They can be opened and closed within 24 hours but in a separate trading session.

Research supports holding trades overnight, as gains made from the close to the next day's open have been shown to be greater than just holding from the day's open to the day's close.

Also, if this is a stock or ETF you're worried about owning overnight for any reason, it may be the wrong time to be trading that particular security and might be better off left alone.

3. Trade with a cash account.

Most brokers allow you to choose the type of account, cash or margin. While margin accounts offer greater flexibility and buying power, a cash account allows you to trade only with available cash, and you must wait for funds to settle before trading again.

Cash accounts come with their own potential issues, such as Cash Liquidation Violations, Good Faith Violations, and Free Riding Violations, all of which extend beyond Pattern Day Trading violations and are easily avoided with margin accounts.

It's likely that beginning traders will encounter at least one of these issues over their trading career. This is normal, and good brokers typically warn their clients in advance to prevent repeated mistakes that could lead to account locks.

The key is to be aware and learn how to trade within the rules instead of attempting to outsmart the system. The information above applies to both options and stock trades.

Your best strategy is to stick to a plan and work towards building up your equity to a point where you don't have to worry about these restrictions anymore.

Conclusion

The pattern day trading rule was established to assist smaller account investors by limiting the potential damage they could inflict on their portfolio at any given time.

While it might be frustrating for novice traders, these rules can be beneficial, prompting traders to adopt more strategic approaches in deploying capital and executing trades.

The market consistently offers opportunities to trade stocks, but failure to adhere to the rules may leave you sidelined when the best moves occur because you didn't utilize the three ways to avoid pattern day trading problems outlined in this guide!

Chapter 9

**The Definitive Guide to
3 Easy Ways to BLOW UP Your Account**

3 Ways to Take Your Account to Zero! (And Why You Should Avoid Them)

Foreword

This chapter is a compilation of personal experiences I've had while learning to trade. The reality is that most traders fail; it's a fact. Statistics suggest that approximately 90% of new traders blow up their accounts (meaning they take their accounts to zero) within the first year of trading.

I've been there—twice.

A burning desire to learn how to trade fueled me. While I anticipated highs, I didn't expect the emotional lows that came with trading.

In this chapter, I aim to share some of the lessons I've learned, paying my trading tuition. Naturally, I want you to succeed in trading, and by sharing these lessons, I hope to contribute to your success by helping you avoid the same mistakes I made.

Christopher M. Uhl, CMA

Introduction

This is the definitive guide to learning about three easy ways to blow up your account (*heavy sarcasm intended*).

Yes, I said "blow up," and trust me, it's not a good thing.

To "blow up your account" essentially means that you had money, you've lost money, and now you have no money.

That's definitely not something I want you to do. I'm going to share three easy ways to do it, and I'm also going to give you three ideas that might help, so you aren't searching for pennies under the couch.

Blowing up your account is actually pretty normal. I have not met a single trader who hasn't blown up their account at least once. It's remarkably easy to do when you don't understand the risks associated with trading.

I learned from those experiences, and that's the real key here. You're going to face challenges that test your mental fortitude, and if you can figure out how to learn from those quickly, you should be able to turn around and make profitable trades.

Trading Too Big

The first way to blow up your account (definitely the easiest) is trading too big. I have certainly been guilty of that way more times than I want to admit.

Let's say, for example, you have a $10,000 account, and you want to risk it all in one trade because you are very confident that gold is going to go up.

If you've been following the How To Trade Stocks and Options Podcast for any stretch of time, you know I've talked about my gold trade (how it's by far the worst trade I've ever made).

So, you've got a $10,000 account, and you want to double it. Hey, it's easy to do, right!?! That's what people talk about all the time on the internet. It's possible for you, but highly unlikely. So, don't take your $10,000 and think you're going to turn it into millions of dollars by the end of the next 60 days or so. It's just not going to happen. If it does happen, you've taken on extraordinary amounts of risk.

Leveraging up your portfolio and making large trades is not conducive to long-term trading. I try to keep my trades extremely small. I mean, I trade smaller now than I ever have before.

Trading too big can cause significant problems. Concentrating all your efforts on one trade is trading too big, risking a lot to potentially make a lot, or potentially lose a lot. If you can spread that risk across numerous trades, you can maintain a high win rate, and even with some losing trades, it hopefully won't blow up your account.

If you risk only 1% on any one trade, it's just one trade in the next hundred. This way, you're not overly concerned about a single trade going south and wiping out your entire account.

Trading Options without Knowing How

The next way to blow up your account is by trading options when you don't know how to trade options.

Now, I trade options. I love options, but I've also studied them for several years. It's not something I jumped into right away. Now with a long option, let's say that you want to go long at Amazon, and you have bought $10,000 worth of Amazon long calls; you want Amazon to go up.

What if Amazon goes down, stays exactly where it is, or it doesn't go to the call strike that you bought?

All of that $10,000 is gone - every penny of it.

It's not like - Oh! Amazon went down 5%. Oh! That's 5% of my Capital. So, you know it sucks, but I can get over that. No, it's zero.

An option is an all-or-nothing bet. If you're buying options, you want it to go to the strike price plus the amount that you paid for the option in order to break even.

I mean, if you wanted the price of a stock to be below $100.00 and you paid $2.50 for a 100-strike put. Your break-even point is $100.00 - $2.50 = $97.50. So, it has to go not only to the 100 put strike but also has to drop by more than what you paid in order to break even.

You have to be aware of what you're trading. If it doesn't reach your strike price and doesn't surpass what you paid for it, then the trade can potentially be worth nothing. Also, your entire $10,000 portfolio is gone. Let's consider the opposite scenario. If you're selling an option, having sold that hundred-strike put, you want to go long, and your break-even point is the 100-strike minus the credit you've taken.

Let's use the same number, $2.50. If it goes below $97.50, it's a losing trade. Selling options is a high-probability setup. The price of the underlying stock can go up, down to $97.50, or stay exactly where it's at, and you'll still be profitable at expiration.

But just like buying options, there's a point where you won't make any money with selling options. Once it goes past your break-even point, it could potentially fall to zero.

If it does, you're on the hook for not only what's in your account but it's very possible you may owe more than what's in your account (if your broker does not take action to avoid this happening on your behalf).

So, the second way to blow up your account is by buying or selling options. Due to their leverage, they are incredible financial instruments, but they require a steep learning curve. If you don't understand how they work, it can quickly blow up your account.

Not Having a Written Entry and Exit Plan in Place

The third way to blow up your account is probably what happens to most new traders here. First, they started by going too big on their positions, then they started using options when they didn't know how. Now, they don't have an entry and exit plan or maybe even any stop-losses. They're just putting it on and hoping for the best.

I know I've been there. I mean, you have got to find a set of entry criteria that works for you. Maybe it's only putting trades on when certain moving averages cross. Perhaps, it's only putting trades on if the implied volatility rank is above a certain percentile. Maybe it's when the cow jumps over the blue moon...

Whatever the case may be, you've got to figure out an entry plan that works for you and has shown through research and backtesting to be profitable.

In addition, you have to have an exit plan. You need to know your profit targets.

If the target is the price of the underlying asset, maybe it's $105, or maybe it's the profit on the option that you sold. Maybe you're looking to get 50% of max profit. Perhaps, it's an option you bought, and you're trying to achieve a 50% return on capital here.

Whatever the case may be, you need to have entry and exit criteria written down.

Hold yourself accountable to them because, at the moment, you're going to see what you want to see, and it may not actually be what the market is giving you.

I've been there for sure, watching the ticks go by and thinking, "Oh, this looks bearish..." Then, all of a sudden, it goes up. "It looks bullish!" Then, all of a sudden, it goes down. Then, you're stuck with it when you could have said, "If I had followed my plan, I wouldn't have these problems. I'm just trading my plan."

Trading your plan (once you find a plan that works for you) is the easiest way to trade because you know when you get in and when you get out. Also, hopefully, you have found a plan that will be profitable.

I don't want you to blow up your account. Please learn from my mistakes, and you won't have to pay the same amount of "trader tuition" I did to learn these lessons.

Conclusion

No trader has a 100% win rate. I don't care what any person says on social media or on any YouTube video pre-roll ad.

Losing trades are part of the game.

Put yourself in the shoes of a bank. The bank makes money on the money it loans out. Some people buy their $90,000 Range Rover and pay it off during the 72 months they've financed it; some people pay it off early, then some people never pay, and the bank has to write off those loans.

You've got to have enough winning trades to be able to write off the losing ones without the losing ones leading to a large destruction in the capital. Banks usually have about a 1%-3% write-off rate over the course of a year depending on credit standards. If you could do that with your trading and have a 97%-99% success rate, you would be one of the greatest traders ever! (But it's probably not going to happen.)

The key here is risk management, that's how the banks continue to turn profits even when they have to write off the occasional $90,000 deadbeat who didn't pay his bills.

It's human nature to cut winners short to book profits and let losers run, hoping they'll turn around. That's where having your written plan in place will help keep you mechanical and hopefully lead you to a better system that yields better returns.

Chapter 10

**The Definitive Guide to Trading
the Yield Curve**

How to Take Advantage of
the Changes in the Fed
Funds Rate

Foreword

Most people would have no idea what the yield curve is, but you're not like most people, and that's why you're reading this book.

Most people have no idea how to buy or sell bonds, or how their pricing is inverse to interest rates, but, like I said, you're not like most people.

Topics like this get me very excited. It's like a hidden gem that I just found. In fact, one of the largest diamonds in America came from the mud stuck on a tractor's tire in Murfreesboro, Arkansas.

Trading the yield curve can be exciting and potentially lucrative if you get it right. The bond market is exceptionally liquid, meaning you'll find a lot of action there.

This is not your Grandpa's savings bond he bought in 1947; this is real bond trading, and here is exactly how I like to trade changes to the yield curve.

Enjoy!

Christopher M. Uhl, CMA

Introduction

In this guide, we will show you how to trade changes in the yield curve. No matter when you read this, the same principles will apply, although prices may differ.

This guide also emphasizes choosing the right strategy when placing options trades. The market must meet specific conditions to place a Debit Spread versus a Credit Spread, as outlined in this guide.

How to Trade the Yield Curve

The yield curve is flattening, indicating that the percent return on US Government bonds is increasingly becoming more similar, regardless of duration.

When investing in an asset, you would expect to make more return for the longer amount of time it's under the other party's control. You could even think of it as car insurance; your six-month policy at GEICO is going to cost less than the 12-month policy because there is a longer amount of time that your car is being insured.

As of June 27, 2018, the difference between the 10-year (2.83%) and the 2-year (2.52%) notes is only 0.31% or 31 basis points. That's only 31 additional cents on every 100 dollars invested for the additional 8 years.

This curve flattening is even worse when comparing the 10-year note (2.83%) to the 30-year bond at 2.97%. The difference between the two is only 14 basis points. So, for 20 additional years of having your capital tied up, you would earn on average 14 additional cents for every 100 dollars invested.

TLT (iShares 20+ Year Treasury Bond ETF) is one way to look at trading the yield curve.

While it doesn't translate directly to the spreads mentioned above, it does track the longer duration bond prices, which are inverse to interest rates.

So, if you think long-term bond rates will go higher, then you would want to go short TLT; but if you think long-term rates are going to further close the gap to the shorter-term rates, then you would want to go long TLT.

TLT's option prices are currently suppressed, independent of its market price of $122.11. TLT's implied volatility rank is only at 8, indicating that the option prices are only 8% as high as they've been over the last year.

With these prices, a Debit Spread would be optimal as we can take advantage of market direction and a potential increase in option prices.

Conversely, if TLT's option prices were higher, then a Credit Spread would make more sense. A Credit Spread involves selling a position, whereas a Debit Spread involves buying a position. Debit Spreads are best in low implied volatility because prices are more likely to go up due to their already low levels. The opposite is true in high implied volatility, where prices are higher, and Credit Spreads are sold, taking in a credit.

The principle here is to buy low and sell high, guiding the choice of the right strategy for the market conditions.

If you anticipate that long-term bond rates will rise, pushing off the trend and steepening the yield curve, then you could consider buying a Put Debit Spread.

By buying the 122 Put and selling the 124 Put, it establishes a short position in bonds and has a probability of profit of 56%. TLT can go up to $122.75, and this trade would still profit.

Even more crucial, if the option prices rise, this trade could potentially profit even if the breakeven is breached. Debit spreads are optimally suited to take advantage of rising option prices. This trade has a max profit of $75 and a max risk of $125.

But if you anticipate that the yield curve will continue to flatten, pushing down longer-term rates even further, closing the gap to short-term rates and potentially creating an inversion (where shorter-term rates are higher than longer-term rates), then we would look to go long TLT with a Call Debit Spread. By buying the 120 Call and selling the 122 Call, this trade has a 58% probability of profit and a breakeven of $121.19 with a max profit of $81 and a max risk of only $119.

To achieve these types of dollar returns, you would have to buy (or sell) 100 shares of TLT, which would cost as much as $12,211 without margin. However, by using options, we can make trades that have a greater than 50/50 probability of profit and fit these trades into any size portfolio.

TLT is the most liquid bond ETF and has the most liquid options market, making it a great vehicle if you're looking to trade the yield curve.

Conclusion

The Fed Funds rate is set by the Federal Reserve. This is an overnight rate for banks to lend to each other and to the Federal Reserve, and vice versa. When the Fed Funds rate changes, it sends shockwaves across the entire US Treasury yield curve.

As the Fed raises rates, shorter-term rates rise in tandem. This makes shorter-term yields more attractive than they initially were, driving up demand.

The demand has to come from somewhere, and that's from the longer-term dated points on the yield curve. As described above, why would I want to tie up my money for 14 more cents on each $100 for 20 additional years?

The rates for treasury securities are set by the market, buying and selling their positions. Rates and prices are inversely correlated.

Think of it like supply and demand. If the supply is low, demand for that supply is high. If supply is high, then the demand is low.

If the price is low, that's because there's a lot of supply and little demand, pushing rates higher, trying to offer investors a reason to take the bonds.

Conversely, if the price of a bond is high, then the demand for that bond is high, but investors are taking smaller and smaller rates in order to capture the higher price.

Remember that bond trading is mainly due to the price of the bond, not the rate of the bond. Many bond traders will not be in the position long enough to have received the income from the bond in the first place; they're trying to take advantage of the price change, similarly to taking advantage of a dividend-paying stock's price movements.

Chapter 11

**The Definitive Guide to Trading
Like a Casino**

How To Utilize The Exact
Same Strategy As A Casino
In Your Own Portfolio

Foreword

This is one of those things where, when I learned how it worked, I was in shock. Yes, it's 100 percent true. You can utilize the exact same strategy casinos use to build massive billion-dollar empires in your own portfolio.

Now remember, they are playing on a massive scale with tens of millions of dollars exchanging hands constantly. And also remember, the casino does payout and has losers, but it's the scale of how they operate that makes them successful.

Christopher M. Uhl, CMA

Introduction

In this guide, we will cover how to structure trades so they have a similar outcome to how a casino takes in bets and pays out winners, keeping the losing bets as profit - remember, the house always wins.

Be sure to always manage your risk in trading. This is NOT a guarantee that you will be an overnight millionaire, not by any stretch. If people did not win at the casino, nobody would bother trying. The casino makes money because the volume of bets it takes in is larger than the volume of winners paid out.

How to Trade Like a Casino

As the saying goes, "The house always wins." Imagine if you could trade like a casino.

What if you could be the house? Well, this theory is entirely how options trading is based.

An options buyer has the potential to make unlimited gains, just like if you were to hit the jackpot, but it's not the slot machine players who are building billion-dollar empires; it's the casinos.

Why is that?

The casinos set the rules and know the statistical outcomes long before you ever step onto the gambling room floor.

You too can structure your trading portfolio in this way.

By selling out-of-the-money options, you're essentially selling lottery tickets to anyone looking to buy for the chance to win big.

You don't have to own the option first in order to sell it. You're just taking the risk for the opportunity to keep the credit taken in on the trade; essentially, you're collecting the bets placed by the options buyers.

An options seller has potentially unlimited losses, just like the casino does, but the smart options seller knows how to put the odds in their favor.

When you sell options, you set the stakes. You can determine when you sell the option and when to walk away from the trade.

The best options setups are in a high implied volatility environment. High implied volatility means that the options prices are higher than they normally are. You can actually get farther away from the current price of the stock and collect as much or more premium on the sale.

In a low implied volatility environment, a 25 delta put has a 75 percent probability of profit to the options seller. The put may sell for only 50 cents and be only 5 strikes from the current price.

In a high implied volatility environment, a 25 delta put still has the same probability of profit to the seller but maybe 10 strikes away from the current price and be worth 75 cents.

Just like a casino, you're setting the stakes for when you want to make the trade to be the most in your favor. The ladder of these two options is further away from the current price and has a higher premium, making it more advantageous to the seller.

Now you've got to limit your losses. A casino has table limits and they know just how big the jackpot will be.

Just like a losing trade, the amount of bets taken in will be paid out to the occasional winners. But the losses on a short options trade can go on indefinitely unless a stop is put in place.

By buying a further out-of-the-money option than was sold, you're still taking in a credit, you're still trading like a casino, but now you've put a limit on how much the buyer could win from you.

You've set the jackpot and you've set your table limit, now it's just time for the probabilities to play out.

Unlike a casino though, you have much more choice when you play. They're open all day and all night to anyone who walks in. Your portfolio is your hard-earned money and should only be risked when you feel that the reward justifies the position when the chips are stacked in your favor.

Conclusion

The out-of-the-money options that are sold are essentially lottery tickets. The option seller is giving the buyer the opportunity to win big in exchange for taking in a premium upfront.

The buyer has a limited amount of risk, just like buying a lottery ticket, but unlimited earnings potential. This is translated into the seller of the option having unlimited risk but limited profits.

Chapter 12

The Definitive Guide to 60 Second Trading

How to Make a High Probability Options Trade in Only 60 Seconds

Foreword

One of the best things about trading options is that you have the ability to be somewhat wrong in direction yet still profit with the trades.

The high-probability setups that completely shifted my perspective generally have a 60%, 70%, or even 80% probability of profit!

Because of knowing how to make these trades, I can quickly open my portfolio, see what would trigger me to make a trade, and push it through. Once I built the skill to make this happen quickly, I realized it doesn't even take all that long, maybe even 60 seconds!

This guide was adapted from the How to Trade Stocks and Options Podcast titled, "How to Make a High Probability Trade in Only 60 Seconds." If you check out that episode, you'll see that I made the trade in 62 seconds, so this is truly possible once you've mastered the basics and are ready to take your trading game to the next level.

Christopher M. Uhl, CMA

Introduction

In this guide, adapted from the How to Trade Stocks and Options Podcast titled, "How to Make a High Probability Trade in Only 60 Seconds," you'll see exactly, step by step, the process used by professional traders to put on trades with a high probability of success without taking a large amount of time or capital.

This process takes time to master. Please be patient and tread lightly!

Knowing what to do is only half the battle; knowing WHY to put the trade on is much more important than just how.

This guide touches on both the how and the why, so be sure to read to the very end.

Once mastered, these same strategies and principles can be applied to any options trade.

How to Make a High Probability Options Trade
in 60 Seconds

This is the exact process to put on a high-probability trade in 60 seconds using the Tastyworks platform.

Because having mobility and trading fast is one of my most important factors in trading, I'm going to demonstrate how to do this from my iPad. I don't need an 8-monitor trading station; I can do this literally anywhere in the world right from my iPad or my phone.

So first things first, let's start our timer. On your mark, get set... Go!

The first thing I do is come to the grid page, as shown below in Figure 1.

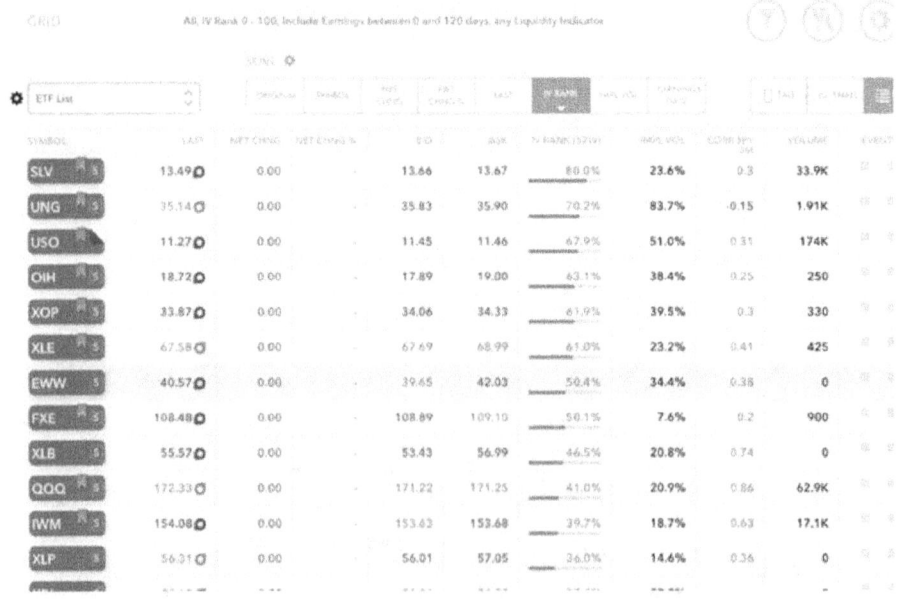

Figure 1

I have already sorted this list in Figure 1 by highest to lowest implied volatility rank. USO, UNG, and SLV are trades that I've already got on. I'm not looking to add any more. So, I'm going to look at EWW.

By clicking on EWW, we are presented with the options chain in Figure 2.

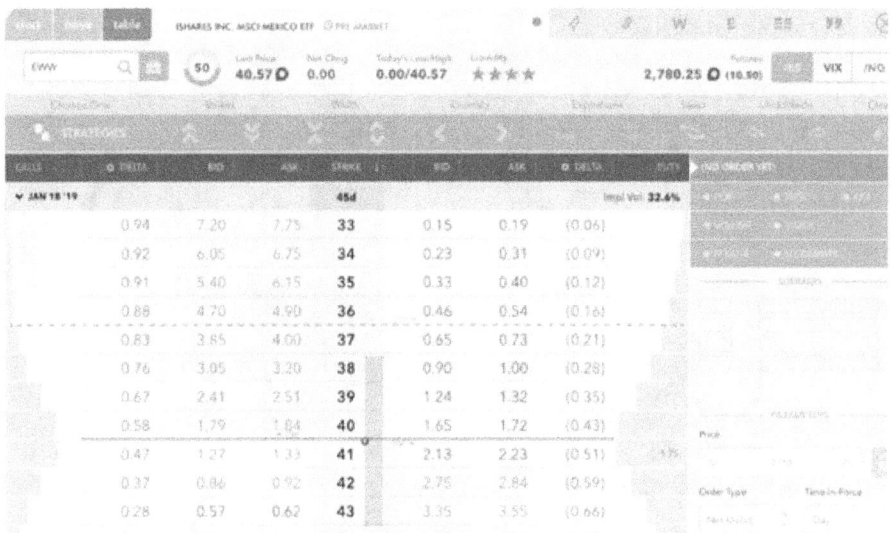

Figure 2

Now, if this is your first time seeing an options chain, I know that it's a lot to look at. I remember the first time I laid eyes on an options chain I literally said, "What do all these numbers mean? I just want to make money?" I understand if it can be a bit overwhelming at the start, but as you gain these trading skills, it becomes second nature.

If you look at the dark blue row, you'll see Calls, Delta, Bid, Ask, Strike, Bid, Ask, Delta, and Puts. What I want you to focus on is the column that says Strike down the middle.

What I want you to focus on is the column that says Delta next to Puts, so on the right half of Figure 2.

See where it says 38? We're going to click the 0.90 on the right-hand side of the 38; this would sell the 38 Delta put. Next, we are going to buy a 37 put by going up one row, clicking the value that says 0.73. Figure 3 shows what the trade screen would look like with both of these two strikes selected.

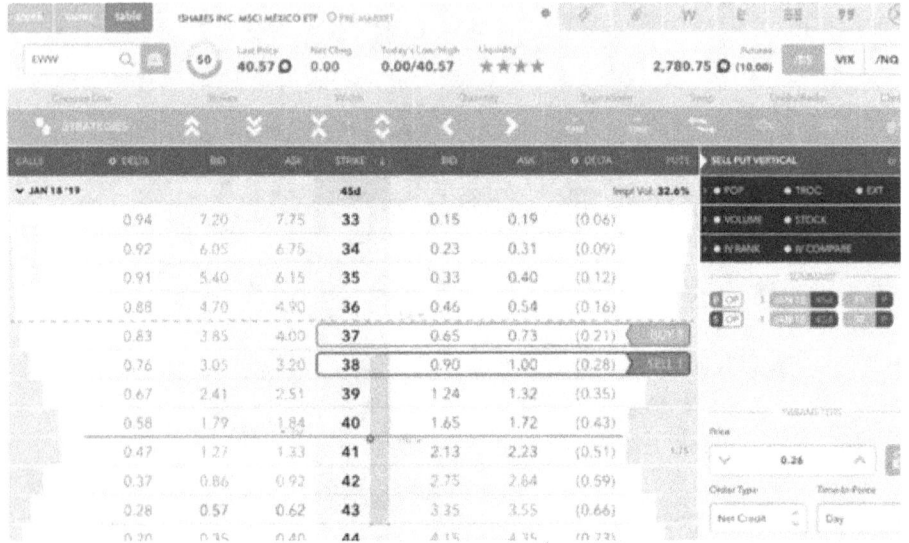

Figure 3

In Figure 3's bottom right, the trade's price is 26 cents in credit, leaving 74 cents for max risk. Calculate the risk by subtracting the credit received (26 cents) from the $1.00 width of the strikes (38-37), resulting in a max risk value of 74 cents.

Tastyworks features a useful trade detail button revealing all trade characteristics, as depicted in Figure 4. The trade exhibits a 72 percent probability of profit, achieved in just one minute and two seconds.

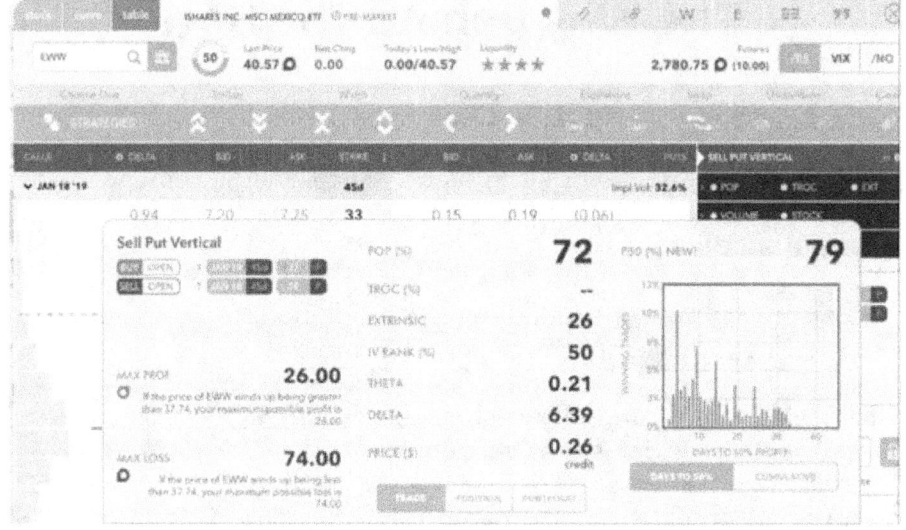

Figure 4

Just send the order, and it's on its way!

The Why Behind The How

The process of executing trades is quite simple, as demonstrated earlier. Clicking about six times can lead to a high probability trade. However, understanding the rationale behind clicking those specific buttons for this high probability trade setup is far more crucial than the execution itself.

The entire trade, from initiation to completion, took a total of 62 seconds. Let's delve into the reasons behind this.

After selecting an underlying stock, such as EWW in this case, the first aspect I consider is the Delta column.

Delta represents the approximate probability of profit for the trade.

You would examine the Delta to determine the probability of profit for being in the money. While being in the money is advantageous for an options buyer, it is not favorable for an options seller. In our scenario of selling the 38 put, being in the money is undesirable.

Since we are selling the 38 put, our goal is for it to expire out of the money, or at least remain out of the money long enough for the premium to decay.

In Figure 5, observe the Delta column on the right half of the options chain. The value (0.28) indicates a 28 percent probability of this strike being in the money at expiration.

Remember, option buyers prefer the strike to be in the money, while options sellers prefer it to be out of the money.

Figure 5

In Figure 5, a 28 percent probability of the strike being in the money implies a 72 percent probability of a profitable outcome, namely being out of the money upon expiration and expiring worthless. The option seller, which is us in this case, would retain all the profit.

Selling just the 38 strike would yield a credit of 90 cents, as indicated under the bid column heading.

However, I always, without question, define my risk in a trade. Selling the 38 put without clearly defining your risk could lead to potentially significant losses.

Therefore, I'm going to buy the 37 put in addition to selling the 38 put. This action reduces the total potential profit in the trade from $90 to $26.

Now, I understand you might be wondering, "Why settle for 26 cents in credit when I could get 90 cents?"

The reason is that the trade would require about $800 in margin. I wanted to clarify that point quickly.

By defining the risk through buying the 37 put, we're only exposing ourselves to a $74 risk on the trade, as opposed to the $800 without risk definition.

Moreover, the return on capital for this trade would be a substantial 35% ($26/$74=35%), significantly higher than the 11% return from selling the 38 put with $800 in margin. This approach not only allows for more trades with similar returns but, most importantly, provides peace of mind.

In my early days of options trading, the unlimited risk associated with stocks kept me up at night. Defining risk helps me stay calm and enables me to engage in more trades.

By limiting the trade risk to $74, I can execute numerous similar trades in my portfolio without tying up excessive capital. I could potentially make 10 more trades with the same amount of capital, resulting in a potential return of approximately $286 on a risk of $814, as opposed to $90 on $800 risked.

That's how you execute a high probability trade in 60 seconds. Simply choose the security, click the trade button, select the option to buy or sell (or both), ensure the Deltas align with your desired probability of profit, review the trade on the trade review page, then hit send. And that's it.

Conclusion

As evident, the "how" of executing trades is genuinely straightforward—it involves pressing a few buttons and sending the order. The statistics reveal that 90% of traders experience account blow-ups and quit within the first year, likely because the act of clicking buttons is deceptively easy.

Options trading is remarkable as it provides traders with a multitude of tools and strategy diversification. The example presented here illustrates a put spread, a small trade with a maximum return on capital of 35%! Compare that to buying the stock outright, where a 35% increase might take a considerable amount of time if it occurs at all. With options trading, we have a 72% probability of achieving such returns in just a few weeks.

Chapter 13

**OVTLYR: The World's Best AI
Stock Trading Assistant**

This is How to Take The Guesswork Out of Trading

Alright, so picture this: You're probably feeling a lot like this little girl right here by the time I finish explaining all about options trading.

People often say it's like trying to drink from a fire hose, and that's the whole deal with learning this new world of trading and investing. It's about mastering the art and skills of trading ahead of time, so you're strategically in the market *only when it makes sense and when there are real opportunities*. Strategically knowing when to hold cash and when to be aggressive is what separates the best from the rest.

Quick question for you - would you like my help to incorporate this into your daily routine? I'm all about helping you integrate the trader lifestyle into your way of life. Imagine getting the golden ticket to the life you've been dreaming about, that is what it's like when you're an OVTLYR trader, just like us.

What is OVTLYR Trading? When you're an OVTLYR Trader (pronounced *Outlier*) you are using the World's Best AI Stock Trading Assistant - taking everything we showed you in this book and then executing a solid trading plan with Artificial Intelligence that helps predict price trends. You'll know when to strategically enter the market, when to get out and when to hold cash - and most importantly - you'll know "Why Outliers Win!"

Imagine getting into the swing of things right away! How great would it be to have someone look over your shoulder at your portfolio every single day, telling you what's working, what's not, and how to handle it? That's exactly what you get with OVTLYR!

But hey, nothing matters if the market isn't playing ball. So, every day, we kick things off with our daily market analysis - top to bottom. That's the OVTLYR trader way. Because, truth be told, practically nothing works if you're trading against the market.

I always tell our traders that trading is like a video game - think Mario. Sometimes you get hit by those stupid little turtles and it's game over, but sometimes you are in the flow, avoiding all the obstacles and evil mushrooms and rescuing the princess. But nothing matters if you don't grasp the trading psychology behind knowing how to navigate the trading obstacles. And we unravel the intricacies of that every single day in our daily trading room with our daily trading psychology sessions.

Dealing with the psychology bit every day is crucial for moving the needle forward. And that's exactly why we have a dedicated trading room inside of OVTLYR, so we can trade together. Everything we do, we do together. No one's left out in the cold, nobody is left out in the dark, everyone walks away with a solid, strategic plan for the day.

Being an OVTLYR trader means you'll understand the ins and outs of the strategies we employ and why we use them. It's like getting a call from me personally every trading day, and our traders love it. We discuss what we're trading *and why* every single trading day!

And here's the kicker - you can ditch a lot of the noise. Say goodbye to those fake gurus who aren't making you any money. No more wasting hours on YouTube hunting for trade ideas that lead nowhere. Forget scrolling on Twitter, trying to decipher the next YOLO Wall Street bet. We trade everything together!

Now, as a proud member of OVTLYR, you'll get daily video calls for free from me. It's a package deal - daily trade alerts, portfolio updates, market analysis, new trade setups, and a dose of trading psychology. And every other Friday, we have live training Q&A sessions so you'll become a market expert in no time.

We're cooking up new courses, and here's the twist - we're doing it together. I want your input, your questions. We'll discuss and find the best answers, so it's not just me dictating what works. It's a collaborative effort, ensuring you grasp how the market operates today, not just in theory, but in the real world.

You'll witness me personally demonstrating how to apply lessons from the trading courses to your trades. It's like an up-to-the-minute field report from the front lines of trading, guiding you on how to replicate it in your portfolio quickly. The only way you'd get this level of access is if you worked with me every day in my office.

Who's this for? New traders looking to skip the Wall Street tuition, experienced traders adding a new dimension to their strategy, busy professionals juggling life and trading, side hustlers aiming for that extra income, and parents looking to jump start their financial future while the little ones nap.

If you've never traded before, no worries - we've got you covered. We'll walk you through everything you need to step into the game, get ready, and stand on your own two feet. Hope it's cool if I overdeliver...

Now, the big question: If all this did was set you up to see how real traders actually profit in the market, would it be worth it? What if could it shave off years from your learning curve and help you dodge costly mistakes? Would it be worth it? What if it allowed you to model our trades, cutting through the internet noise? Would it be worth it?

What's one perfect trade worth to you? What would you do once you've developed the stock trading skills you've always desired?

Let's break it down. You're getting daily video calls, live training and QA, the full catalog of best-selling courses, and access to chat rooms - everything you need to become a successful trader. But you've got two choices - first, do nothing, and nothing changes. Continue struggling, searching YouTube, and Twitter, and listening to your fake gurus.

Or the second option - invest in yourself, learn how the market really works head to ovtlyr.com, and give it a shot. There's no contract and you can cancel anytime.

I can't wait to see you on the inside! Join us right away at ovtlyr.com and let's get started today! See you there soon!